Message Matters

Succeeding at the Crossroads of Mission and Market

Rebecca K. Leet

FIELDSTONE
ALLIANCE

SAINT PAUL
MINNESOTA

Fieldstone Alliance is committed to strengthening the performance of the nonprofit sector. Through the synergy of its consulting, training, publishing, and research and demonstration projects, Fieldstone Alliance provides solutions to issues facing nonprofits, funders, and the communities they serve. Fieldstone Alliance was formerly Wilder Publishing and Wilder Consulting departments of the Amherst H. Wilder Foundation. For information about other Fieldstone Alliance publications, see the last page of this book. If you would like more information about Fieldstone Alliance and our services, please contact

Fieldstone Alliance
60 Plato Boulevard East, Suite 150
Saint Paul, MN 55107

800-274-6024
www.FieldstoneAlliance.org

Edited by Vincent Hyman
Designed by Kirsten Nielsen
Manufactured in the USA
First printing, August 2007

Library of Congress Cataloging-in-Publication Data

Leet, Rebecca K., 1949-
  Message matters : succeeding at the crossroads of mission and market / Rebecca K. Leet.
    p. cm.
  Includes index.
  ISBN-13: 978-0-940069-63-3
  ISBN-10: 0-940069-63-6
  1. Nonprofit organizations--Management. 2. Charities--Management. 3. Endowments--Management. 4. Associations, institutions, etc.--Management. 5. Corporations--Public relations. I. Title.
  HD62.6.L44 2007
  658'.048--dc22

                                    2007024676

To my parents, Patricia and Julian Leet,
for their lifelong support of independent thinking.

Acknowledgments

IDEAS ARE LIKE BLOOMS: even potent seeds need lots of sun if they are going to flourish. The basic framework that I present in *Message Matters* was a seed in the mid-1990s. Since then, it has grown and developed with the help of innumerable individuals and client organizations.

The list is too long for me to thank everyone, although I would like to. I can, and do, express my gratitude to several who have provided long-term encouragement or especially timely help: John Bissell, Lou Capozzi, Isolde Chapin, Chris DeCardy, Jon Funabiki, the late Jim Gorman, Brian Hanson, Judy Langford, Beth Norcross, Jillaine Smith, and Rebecca Wodder. And I thank Vince Hyman, who is that rare commodity every writer needs: a *good* editor.

A special thanks to Kate Madison for years of helping me work through puzzles and to Denise Cavanaugh for her unfailing support throughout my consulting career.

I also appreciate the generosity of clients who have permitted me to use their experiences as case studies in this book, including the American Lung Association, Arlington Community Foundation, Center for the Study of Social Policy, Juvenile Diabetes Research Foundation International, National Association for the Education of Young Children, Nebraska Health and Human Services System, and ZERO TO THREE.

And then there are the people who are the constant sunshine in my life: my partner Christopher Munford and my daughters Caitlin and Kristin Corcoran. Thank you for helping me flourish in every season.

About the Author

REBECCA K. LEET is principal of Rebecca Leet & Associates, which helps organizations think before they speak and speak so that others listen. She has provided strategic counsel to nonprofits since 1985, often serving organizations that are undertaking a process for the first time. For example, she developed the first strategic plan for Friends of the Earth, the first strategic marketing plan for the American Lung Association, and the first strategic communications plan for ZERO TO THREE.

In addition to consulting, Rebecca writes and speaks about management and communications issues and has been published or quoted in publications ranging from the *Wall Street Journal* to the *Chronicle of Philanthropy* to *PR Week*. She is the author of *From Fundraiser to Change Agent: The Story of Transforming United Way of Metropolitan Atlanta* (United Way of Metropolitan Atlanta, 2003) and *Marketing for Mission* (BoardSource, 1998). She is the former editor of *Strategic Governance for Nonprofit Executives and Boards*.

Rebecca brings a wealth of real-life experience to her consulting, writing, and speaking. Prior to starting her firm, she was a congressional reporter for the *Washington Star*, director of news information for ABC News/Washington, press secretary to former U.S. Senator Lowell Weicker, and vice president of communications for the Wilderness Society. She has served on numerous boards of directors, locally and nationally, and was the founding president of two nonprofits in her hometown of Arlington, Virginia. She is currently on the board of directors of the Public Leadership Education Network (PLEN) and the George Foster Peabody Awards, which are the nation's highest awards for broadcast, cablecast, and webcast programming.

Rebecca can be reached online at www.leetassociates.com.

Contents

Introduction 1

1. The Power of the Message 5

2. What Is a Strategic Message? 13

3. The Core Principles of Strategic Messages 31

4. Step One: Identify the Action Desired 41

5. Step Two: Identify the Target Audiences 55

6. Step Three: Identify Audience Desires 63

7. Step Four: Find the Mutuality 79

8. Step Five: Express the Message 85

9. Putting the Steps Together:
    The Process of Message Development 95

10. A Case Study: The Power of Strategic Messages 107

11. Other Applications
    of the Strategic Message Framework 127

Conclusion 137

Appendix 141
    Organizational Needs Assessment 141
    Organizational Readiness Assessment 142

Endnotes 143

Index 145

Introduction

TODAY'S WORLD RUNS at the speed of a mouse click. Click: my document opens. Click: the Internet appears. Click: here's my e-mail. Click: everything disappears. We expect information to arrive in seconds, satisfy our specific desire, and be gone so we can move on.

Technology is conditioning us to expect humans to deliver satisfaction at click-speed also. Click: what does your organization do? Click: what are the organization's top three priorities? Click: what does principled multi-lateralism mean? Click: tell me about the new project you're launching. If we falter in delivering in a few seconds, *click*, we disappear because our audience has moved on.

Being heard today demands delivering information quickly and clearly, but even that is not enough. Being heard also demands delivering the information *that resonates with your audience's desires* quickly, clearly, and continually. In other words, being heard depends on delivering a strategic message. If you don't, *click*, your audience will be gone.

Today, being heard demands delivering the information that resonates with your audience's desires quickly, clearly, and continually.

Message Matters is designed to serve leaders of associations, nonprofit organizations, and foundations across all sectors who ask the same question: when we are talking about issues of such importance, why aren't people listening? It tells organizations why to adopt the framework of strategic message development and how to apply the methodology so they connect more successfully with their target audiences and compel these audiences to action. It shares the experiences of more than a dozen associations, nonprofit organizations, foundations, and government agencies that have advanced their causes by using strategic messages. They are organizations that are trying to cure diabetes, adopt best professional practices, prevent child abuse, deliver government services more effectively, change American journalism, and rebuild communities. Moving people to action is essential to achieving the mission of most nonprofit organizations and should be the goal of most of their organizational decision making and communication.

This book assumes a medium- or large-sized organization with several program areas and a department (of one or more staff) whose duties include fundraising, marketing, communications, or all three. The approach described in the book, however, is equally useful to smaller nonprofits with budgets of less than two million dollars and a staff smaller than ten because

- The need to create and use strategic messages is as great for small organizations as for larger ones.

- The framework for thinking about why and how to approach developing a strategic message is the same for an organization with two staff members as it is for an organization with two hundred staff members.

- The five-step process for creating a strategic message is the same for organizations of any size.

- The need to involve people with different perspectives or expertise in the process is the same for all organizations, although smaller organizations may need to inlcude people outside their staff to accommodate this need. A medium or large organization usually taps staff and a board member or two to serve on a strategic message development team. Smaller organizations are more likely to fill out a team by enlisting more board members or asking volunteers, clients, professional colleagues, or even friends.

Message Matters introduces the Action Connection, an innovative framework for strategic decision making, and applies it to creating strategic messages using a simple five-step process. Throughout the book are case studies of organizations that have created strategic messages using this framework and process. (The Action Connection framework can be used to make a variety of other strategic decisions: designing new programs, increasing fundraising effectiveness, filtering new ideas, and increasing management effectiveness. More about this is explained in the final chapter.)

Understanding the framework behind the message development process is important. It helps an organization grasp how a strategic message differs from similar-sounding products like a brand, a frame, or an elevator speech. It grounds the message development work in value assumptions that discipline how the process plays out.

Following the framework discussion, the book carefully explains the five steps to developing a strategic message. It then describes a tested methodology for executing the steps: one that has been used repeatedly with organizations of varying sizes and goals. There follows a chapter that brings the theory and process to life in a case study explaining how strategic messages helped an organization launch and build a nationwide movement to change the paradigm for preventing child abuse. If you're wondering whether you *need* to develop a strategic message and whether you are *ready* to undertake message development, turn to the appendix before you begin; there you will find a ten-question needs assessment and a seven-question readiness assessment.

The concepts and approach explained in this book build on years of work across the spectrum of professional communications and address the everyday challenges of twenty-first-century organizations. Like all business executives' careers today, mine has unfolded during one of the greatest communication revolutions of human history. I began my professional life as a newspaper reporter in Washington, DC, during the Watergate era—a time when newsrooms were converting from manual typewriters to computers and from sending typesetters stories glued page-to-page to transmitting stories electronically. Following that, I served as press secretary to a U.S. senator. In those days, we actually put out double-sided press releases on legal-sized paper—and reporters actually read them. By the time I became a vice president for communications of a national environmental group, competition for reporters' eyes had reached the point where we needed to be much more strategic in what we released and how and when we released it: shorter releases with lots of bulleted bits, localized if possible, preceded and followed by phone calls to argue our case for coverage.

In the ensuing two decades of consulting, I have watched as catching some-one's eye and ear has become more and more difficult. To continue the reporter example, in the early 1980s one could be pretty sure of having the headline and first paragraph of a press release read by a reporter. Later in the decade, it dropped to just the headline and the first sentence. In the 1990s, it became just the headline. Then distribution switched to e-mail; the sub-ject line had to be brief and captivating if you hoped for further reading. Now, all too often, if the name in the e-mail address isn't recognized, the subject line is irrelevant. Any professional communicator, regardless of spe-cialty, could tell a similar story.

No one today is untouched by the communication revolution. It seems im-possible to find a quiet sanctuary, somewhere protected from the constant barrage of information. We are bombarded with so much communication so constantly that it feels, at times, like a physical assault. Most of us have begun, consciously or unconsciously, to protect ourselves by turning a blind eye and a deaf ear. Society is reaching the point where the more we are told, the less we hear.

Society is reaching the point where the more we are told, the less we hear. Unanswered, this challenge promises nothing but decline for associations, nonprofits, and foundations that are trying to serve families, workers, and communities.

Unanswered, this challenge promises nothing but decline for nonprofits, associations, and foundations that are trying to serve American families, workers, and communities. Communication is the basis for all coopera-tive action and an essential ingredient in making change, which is the pri-mary product of nonprofit organizations. In this environment, success—even survival—requires associations and nonprofits to communicate in new ways. To evolve, these organizations' most critical capacity is the ability to create and deliver strategic messages.

1. The Power of the Message

MOST AMERICANS FIRST HEARD the term "the message" in connection with the president of the United States: *The president stayed on message today about changes in the Social Security system.* To some, that association with the president implies that messaging is done only at extraordinary levels by extraordinarily important people.

That's wrong. It's done at extraordinary levels because it is so important, which is the same reason that it needs to be done at ordinary levels by ordinary people.

The president of the United States spends part of every day focused on his message because he is trying to change the world. There are close to 1.5 million presidents of nonprofit organizations in the United States, most of whom are also trying to change some part of the world. Yet very few spend part of the year, much less the day, focused on their message.

One has to wonder: if "the message" is important enough for the president of the United States to work on every day, why isn't it important enough for the president of the city's free clinic, the state bar association, or the National Coalition to Save the Mongoose?

The answer, of course, is that it *is* just as important. And it is important for the same reason: in an age of information overload and nanosecond transmission, the message determines whether you are heard and people respond.

In today's world, conversations are born—and most die—in the first fateful minute of contact. Yet most professionals in the nonprofit world, who can easily talk for thirty minutes about their work, are unable to talk for just thirty seconds. This inability is fatal.

Those who can connect quickly enough to survive the first seconds often fail later because they get caught up in their own agenda and forget to maintain contact with the listener's interests. In an era of increasing personal power, people have a "me" orientation, and they quickly tune out information that no longer speaks to their concerns.

Strategic messages help executives meet the triple challenge of information overload, instant communication, and increased personal power. A *strategic message* does three things: it captures the attention of a target audience, it drives the conversation with that audience, and it results in action both the organization and the individual want. Mutual satisfaction is the key to successful messaging.

Results and Benefits of a Strategic Message

Mutual satisfaction between the organization and its target audiences is the key to successful message development. You will know you've been successful when your strategic message yields the following results:

1. It captures the attention of a target audience.

2. It drives the conversation with that audience.

3. It results in action *both* the organization and the individual want.

Furthermore, the *process* of developing a strategic message also yields three benefits for the organization:

1. It gives everyone in the organization simple, persuasive, and memorable words that express the essence of the organization (or project) to stakeholders.

2. It sharpens the organization's understanding of its own goals or a project's goals and their value to both the organization and its stakeholders.

3. It helps the organization internalize the knowledge that the organization (or project) delivers different value to different constituents; therefore, satisfying varied stakeholder desires may require strategic change in program design, resource allocation, or internal operations.

A strategic message not only supports speakers in surviving the first fateful minute of a conversation, it helps structure the ensuing conversation so that the speaker stays focused both on the action he or she wants *and* on how that action overlaps with what the listener wants. It helps the speaker avoid wandering off and talking about things that are less important.

Some would argue that technology, not message, determines whether one is heard in today's oversaturated environment. Indeed, incessant changes in communication technologies over the past decade have drawn nonprofit executives to focus on technological currency as the key to effective communication. Many have become physically and fiscally exhausted trying to keep up with technological change. However, many are now realizing that they have overemphasized delivery and underemphasized content—that is, message. Too often these nonprofit executives discover they have hot technology that leaves their audiences cold.

The Challenges: Overload and Speed

One reason that strategic messages grow more important daily is because the volume of communications bombarding each of us is growing, as is the speed with which it comes at us. While we all recognize this, it is helpful to pause and take in the enormity of the communications challenge facing every individual today:

Historic Magnitude. We are living through the fourth major communication revolution of human history, as computer prophet Ithiel de la Sola Pool foresaw. More than 20 years ago, he wrote that computer communication is as fundamental a change as the advent of writing 5,000 years ago, the advent of printing 500 years ago, and the advent of the telegraph (progenitor of the telephone, radio, and television) 150 years ago.[1] Small wonder that yesterday's tried-and-true solutions don't seem to work anymore.

Inconceivable Volume. The knowledge base doubles every two years.[2] If all the *new* information being stored each year were reduced to print, housing it would require building a *half-million* new libraries the size of the Library of Congress print collection *annually*.[3] How do you educate target audiences when information changes so fast?

Inhuman speed. It took thirty years for radio to reach sixty million people. It took fifteen years for television to do the same. It took the Internet only three years.[4] And, within one decade of the Internet becoming generally available to the public (in 1994), two-thirds of American homes, 95 percent of public libraries, and virtually all public schools were hooked up[5]—not to mention government at all levels and most companies. Our world is being transformed at a speed that makes it impossible to keep up, and no one knows how long it will continue.

Ceaseless Responding. Researcher M. Rex Miller estimates that we are now expected to respond to the world with a speed similar to that required of fighter pilots in combat, whose decision making allows "little or no time for reflection in an environment that changes at high speed in an irregular, disorderly, and unpredictable manner."[6] Fighter pilots, however, get a rest now and then.

Understandable Consequence. According to a 2005 study by the Institute of Psychiatry at the University of London, workers who are hit incessantly by phone calls, e-mails, and text messages suffer a ten-point decrease in IQ—more than double the drop caused by smoking marijuana.[7] We might be better off if we tuned out and toked.

Overlooked Challenge: Satisfying Desire

Without question, today's speed and volume of communication greatly impede the ability of foundations, associations, and nonprofits to break through to audiences and be heard. However, there is another, often overlooked factor that creates an equally significant barrier when it is not accommodated: personal power. At the heart of strategic message development is the realization that Americans feel increased personal power, and the consequence of such empowerment is that organizations must address audiences' desires if they hope to break through to them and be heard.

Americans today have more and more choices about what they do and how, when, and with whom they do it. The twin sister of choice is control—that is, power. Arguably, Americans have more power over their personal lives than ever before. Although the dizzying speed of change and ensuing chaos may make many feel as though they lack control in their lives, evidence to the contrary is all around us. To cite just a few examples:

We command our entertainment environment. Between iPods, satellite radio, and music webcasting, not to mention the old-fashioned Discman and radios, we can listen to whatever music we desire virtually wherever and whenever we want.

The same is increasingly true with visual entertainment. We access hundreds of cable channels in our family room. Our kids watch DVDs en route to grandma's house. We ship whatever is on our TV, DVD player, or TiVo at home to wherever we are in the world, whenever we want, and watch on our computer, PDA, or cell phone.

At times, we can play one medium off another to get the version of an experience that we want. In 2005, five million people tuned in to AOL's live webcast of the Live 8 concert series, instantly flipping between the concerts in London, Paris, Philadelphia, Toronto, Rome, and Berlin. Those viewers opted for the AOL webcast over the MTV televised version, in which MTV controlled what viewers heard and ran commentators' voices over the music. Without question, those five million AOL viewers were noticed by MTV Network's CEO Judy McGrath, who elsewhere has remarked that viewers want "My MTV…that means a very personal relationship to whatever it is you are interested in."

We are in-control consumers. In 2005, the tagline on General Motors' "BuyPower" web site delivered a clear message to the personally powerful: *Your car. Your choice. Your way.* Nike feels the same way about shoes. For several years, customers have been able to go to NikeID.com and create custom designed shoes for themselves—picking the color, the fabric, and embroidering their name on the side—for only ten dollars more than the price at Sports Authority. For the news consumer, the options are limitless and almost all free. An Akron resident who hungers for a wider view of the world than he gets from the *Akron Beacon Journal* can go to the *Times of London* web site to read about the war in Iraq, the *New York Times* web site to keep current with the arts, and the *Detroit Free Press* web site to read hometown coverage of the Tigers in the World Series. Customer power just keeps growing; the eMiniMall surfaced in 2005 and provided a consumer who was pricing a product on one retailer's web site with comparative prices from other companies without leaving the first site—in essence, the buyer is now so powerful that the good deal comes to her rather than her having to hunt it down.

We are becoming our own news media. Suicide bombers blow up the London subway and the first pictures out are from riders' cell phone cameras. A self-appointed scribe launches an online forum, the Drudge Report, and breaks open a sex scandal that ultimately leads to a president's impeachment. Bloggers reveal the less-than-reliable source of a *60 Minutes* story in the midst of the 2004 presidential election, forcing CBS News to fire an award-winning producer and prompting the retirement of one of the nation's foremost broadcast anchors. And in hundreds of communities across the United States, local newspapers and broadcast stations adopt "civic journalism" practices that encourage greater involvement of citizens in defining news and influencing how it is covered.

We are increasingly powerful workers. No longer tethered by benefits like guaranteed pensions, we do not anticipate working somewhere for decades and employers know they must be flexible to keep the best of us. So we expect a menu of benefits from which to choose. We push for different work hours or telecommuting options to help us avoid arduous commutes or juggle difficult family schedules. We rotate leadership of office work groups. We endure less management hierarchy and make more decisions ourselves. Even the military has devolved decision making. In 1999, the *Washington Post* reported that Marine commanders now must explain the goal of an assignment to troops in less than one written page—it is then up to the troops to decide how to accomplish the assignment.[8] This change reflects the different way in which wars are now fought: not on battlefields alone, but in cities where within a single block soldiers may need to be warriors, police, and social workers all within the same day. Regardless of the sector—whether government, commercial, or nonprofit—success requires giving decision-making authority to workers formerly considered too low on the organizational chart to make independent decisions. And those individuals carry that sense of empowerment—and expectation of choice—into all areas of their lives.

We even define God. Even in the spiritual realm, Americans may be assuming more power: they are increasingly defining God for themselves. A Roper Starch poll in 2000 showed that the number of Americans who believe in God has stayed steady over time at 90 percent. However, the number of those in 2000 who said that no standard definition of God "comes close" to their notion of the Divine had more than doubled since 1980.[9]

The result of increased personal power is that we tend to react adversely when we feel we are not being considered, when our cooperation is taken for granted, or when we are being told what to do or think. If an organization wants to connect with us, we need to see or hear something we care about reflected in its words.

That is what a strategic message does. It speaks so that an organization's audiences hear their desires reflected in the message. The shared desires of an organization and its audiences create the common ground from which spring messages that connect and compel action—messages that can be heard over the din.

If connecting with people today requires connecting to their desires, moving people to action requires letting them hear they'll meet their desire by taking the action. A strategic message does this. The speed with which people connect to an organization is less important than whether their desires are met when they do. The volume of information an organization makes available is less important than whether any of it connects with peoples' interests. Today, successful communications depends less on how fast or how much information a group provides, and more on whether the information delivers something constituents want.

Summary

- If messaging is important enough for the president of the United States to focus on, it's important enough for nonprofit, foundation, and association executives to focus on.

- Strategic messages grow more important daily, as the volume and speed of communications only increase.

- Speed and volume of communications are barriers to being heard, but an overlooked, and perhaps more important, barrier is the increase in personal power, which results in people ignoring whatever does not directly connect to their desires.

Discussion Questions

1. Are we satisfied with how well our most important stakeholders listen to us?

2. Do we focus too much of our energies on *how* we communicate with our audiences—the technology—and not enough on *what* we communicate?

3. Do we ever talk about our strategic message relative to any aspect of our organization?

4. Do we recognize the impact that increased personal power has on all aspects of how we communicate, how we structure our programs, how we manage the organization, or other aspects of our operations?

2. What Is a Strategic Message?

THE MESSAGE—WHAT IS IT?

Professionals in all kinds of organizations and different fields of specialization talk about "the message," but many are unsure exactly what it is. Is it the same as a brand, the word *du jour* for virtually anything in communications? Is it creating a slogan? How does it differ from a frame or an elevator speech? What the heck are we talking about here?

There is no universally accepted definition of a strategic message. Ask the CEO what messaging is and you'll get one answer. Ask the head of public policy and you'll likely get another. Ask the vice president of field operations and you'll get a third. Ask the director of volunteers and you'll get yet another version.

It would be helpful if nonprofit, foundation, and association staff could at least turn to one of their communications professionals and get the definitive answer. But communications professionals vary in their definitions too, and for the same reason: most look at a strategic message through the narrow lens of their own specialty. Someone who deals mainly with the news media will give one answer. A web master will give another. Whoever handles advertising will give you a third. Conference staff, the publications department, the development department, direct mail experts, specialists in soliciting high-income donors, planned giving counselors, foundation grant writers—all are likely to define the term from their own distinct perspectives.

A Strategic Message: Defined

To reduce the confusion of definitions, we'll use the following:

A strategic message is a set of statements that prompts targeted audiences to take a desired action.

Strategic messages are used at any time, by organizations of all kinds, to achieve a diverse array of goals. When a professional association changes its accreditation requirements, it designs a strategic message aimed at members, professional schools, and relevant industries—each of which it wants actively supporting the change, albeit in different ways. When a foundation institutes a requirement that grantees evaluate foundation-funded programs using a designated new process, the foundation crafts a strategic message aimed at grantees, foundation program officers, and nonprofit management professionals—all of whom would need to change the manner in which they do business in varying ways. When an environmental group launches a new campaign to protect a local river, it creates a strategic message targeted at environmentally sensitive consumers, local policymakers, volunteers, and donors—all of whom would need to take some kind of supportive action. When a young membership organization is ready to create an institutional identify, it crafts a strategic message targeted at members, potential members, and others who are important actors in its continued growth because each of those groups would need to have a clear and consistent understanding of the organization.

A strategic message helps these organizations and professionals achieve their goals because it does these three things:

1. *It captures the attention of a target audience.*
   A strategic message breaks through information overload, catching and holding the audience through the first fateful minute of contact.

2. *It focuses the subsequent conversation on attaining mutual desires.*
   A strategic message structures the conversation in such a way that you remain aware of what you want and what your audience wants so that most of your conversation occurs in the area where your desires overlap.

3. *It results in action you both want.*
   By knowing what you want and talking to your audience in terms of what they want, you are more likely to achieve your goal because your audience recognizes that, by acting, they will obtain a desire of their own.

Strategic messages are used by professionals of many different specialties because virtually all professionals are in the business of achieving goals that require other people to act. They are targeted at external or internal audiences of any size or composition, from a handful on a department staff to thousands of activists. They seek to elicit almost any kind of action. For example:

A vice president for membership who is concerned that the association "isn't telling our members what they need to hear" would initiate a strategic message development process and create language designed to help members recognize that the association is giving them what they want and they should keep renewing their membership.

A public policy director who wants Congress to ban snowmobiles from Yellowstone National Park would work with a small group to develop a strategic message that speaks to people with varying kinds of influence—environmental voters, members of Congress, the news media—in a way that helps achieve silence near Old Faithful.

A medical director at a local free clinic who says "we need to find a way to get more kids immunized" is actually saying that the clinic needs to develop a strategic message that will persuade local government and school officials, parents, and pediatricians to take actions that result in more children being vaccinated.

A nonprofit CEO and his board president, who need to increase financial contributions from board members, realize they must think strategically, design a message that appeals to board members' desires and therefore is persuasive, and communicate that message repeatedly and consistently over time until board members recognize the need and meet it.

Core Message, Subset Messages

Although a strategic message is usually referred to singularly as "the message," it is actually a combined message. It includes an overarching *core message* that speaks to the self-interests of all target audiences and a set of *subset messages* for each audience that speaks to the specific desires of that group.

The rationale behind having an overarching core message may not be immediately apparent. Isn't the point of a message to speak as specifically as possible to a target audience? Absolutely. But people move between target audiences, and therefore a core message must overarch all audiences. The same core message must be heard regardless of which audience the person belongs to at any given moment because it is remembered only when it is heard again and again and again.

Here are two examples of how the same person can belong to two different target audiences:

- A staff member from a home health care agency may happily hear the agency's message about reducing Sunday client visits when he hears it as an employee. When he visits his elderly mother and reads the letter that the agency sent her announcing the change, he may feel worried because he reads it from the perspective of a caregiving son. He has different concerns depending on the role that he is in at the moment, and those different concerns might cause him to hear the reasoning behind the change differently. To achieve maximum understanding and retention, the agency's core message needs to be the same each time even though the subset messages will differ in what they emphasize.

- A city council member hears a community group's message about the need for a new school in one way, but when he returns home at night and is in his parental frame of mind, he hears the need in a different way. A consistent core message helps him become increasingly aware that someone thinks there is a need for a new school; it provides a "landing pad" for the subset message aimed at him as a local legislator and the different subset message aimed at him as a father.

Because people frequently belong to more than one audience, the core message must be consistent regardless of when and where it is delivered: at a donor event, in a newsletter, on the promotional brochure for a fundraising walk, in a newspaper story, on a web site, in an e-mail to staff, at a community meeting, and everywhere else. Similarly, subset messages must be consistent in their delivery to target audiences. Consistency and repetition are the foundation for a message being heard, remembered, and, ultimately, acted on.

When I work with strategic messaging clients, I capture and present the messages in a format called a *message matrix*. The matrix displays, in a concise way, the core message and the subset messages for each audience. The fictional example of a completed message matrix below shows the core message that overarches all audiences and the subset messages for each of this organization's three target audiences. As will be addressed in later chapters, the subset messages differ because each speaks directly to a desire of a specific target audience.

Message Matrix for Reading ReachOut

Core message		
We give homeless children the literacy foundation they need to succeed in school: read-aloud experiences, books to keep, and materials to write and draw with.		
Subset messages: Parents	**Subset messages:** Funders	**Subset messages:** Volunteers
One of the best educational gifts you can give your children is free: just encourage them to enjoy books because children who love books do better in school.	Three-quarters of city elementary school teachers have had a Reading ReachOut child in class, and virtually all these teachers report seeing evidence of the program's positive effect on school performance.	Reading ReachOut volunteers choose when they want to work, at what shelter, and with what age child.
One of the best ways to encourage your children's love of books is to share books with them—hold your child on your lap and read or simply talk about the pictures together.	Grants and donations to Reading ReachOut are matched dollar for dollar with public funds because we have been designated one of the city's ten most outstanding community organizations.	Our volunteers find their work so rewarding that 85 percent return each year.
We want to help you however we can in encouraging your children to love books.	We want to expand our reach by increasing the number of shelters we serve from six to ten over the coming two years.	We provide training for all volunteers, and a Reading ReachOut staff member is always available to help with any problems that arise.

Most Common Reasons
to Develop a Strategic Message

There are three situations that commonly lead associations, foundations, and nonprofits to develop a strategic message: (1) they are trying to move a targeted group to take immediate action, (2) they are trying to project a clear institutional identity, and (3) they are trying to describe a complex or technical body of work to nonexpert audiences. More specifically,

1. All strategic messages ultimately seek to effect action, but some are intended to elicit action more directly than others. The most frequent reason for developing a strategic message is to cause action in the near term. An association of financial planners wants members to become activists and help persuade Congress to enact legislation that would benefit the profession. A foundation wants grantees to become more focused on outcome measures. A social service agency wants low-income parents to enroll their children at a neighborhood child care center. Each develops a strategic message to help it achieve its goal.

   Be aware that such messages may actually urge inaction or a cessation of action. Sexual abstinence messages, for example, are strategic messages even though they advocate *not* doing something.

2. An organization or an individual program may develop a strategic message to achieve a clearer identity with its target audiences, usually to support later efforts to activate those constituencies. This is the second most frequent use of strategic messages. A local foundation wants to be understood by the community so it will receive grant proposals in its areas of interest rather than in areas in which it is not involved. A democracy-building program focusing on Latin America wants to differentiate itself from similar programs with a global focus so that the news media will call it first when seeking analysis about developments in that area of the world. A local literacy program wants the community to recognize its distinctive focus on homeless children so that it will be easier to raise funds and attract volunteers when needed. Each develops a strategic message that has an institutional focus to help it distinguish itself in stakeholders' minds.

Moving to Action: New Funders for Journalism Reform

In 1999, one of the seminal efforts to make American journalism more relevant to readers and more supportive of civic life needed new funding. The foundation that had launched and supported the project for a decade was, as planned, ending its ten-year sponsorship.

With constant financial support throughout the project's lifetime, the staff had not needed to divert program time to the task of activating donors. They were innovative journalists, but now they had to be fundraisers and find others who wanted change in journalistic practice. They wondered whom to approach and what to say to them beyond a clearly unsatisfactory reportorial approach: *We need new funding. Will you help?*

The executive director decided that the staff needed a strategic message to use when approaching donor prospects. Staff members were clear about the action they desired: getting money to continue the project. As they identified potential partners who could effect that action, they asked themselves why those organizations might want to support the project. And as they answered that question, they recognized something they had not seen as clearly before: the unique contribution the program was making to journalistic reform. It was, essentially, the only laboratory incubating new ideas for changing traditional practices.

This recognition helped the staff identify potential institutional and individual funders; they were people who valued changing the way news is defined, gathered, and reported in the United States. It also helped the organization develop the language with which to approach their target audiences.

The situation definitely called for developing a strategic message that would prompt near-term action by funders. As with most such messages, the core message did not bluntly demand action. Instead, it opened by asserting a desire shared by the project and prospective donors, and it immediately followed that assertion with implied action. The language of the core message laid the foundation for following quickly with specific and persuasive information for each subset audience.

This was the core message that the program adopted: *American journalism must be transformed today and reinvented for tomorrow. An opportunity exists to ensure the permanent viability of the only laboratory for doing that.*

Sometimes an organization believes that its mission or vision statement is an identity-building strategic message. Wrong. They are different tools and have different uses. The primary purpose of a mission or vision statement is to provide internal direction and to guide decision making, while the primary purpose of a strategic message is to connect with target audiences and move them to action at some point. Mission and vision statements are an expression of what an association, nonprofit, or foundation wants to do or be and are written from the point of view of the organization. Strategic messages are other-focused, that is, oriented to the audience's desires. Although organizations often use mission and vision statements on public documents, they are meant primarily as internal communications and do not serve the same purpose as a strategic message.

3. When an organization wants certain audiences to understand something complex or confusing about its activities—knowledge that is crucial to later supportive action—it develops a message that describes the complex program or idea in a way that strategically connects with the distinct interests of various audiences. This is an important kind of strategic message, but it is developed less often than strategic messages designed to elicit immediate action or raise institutional identity. For example:

- An international association plans to introduce a knowledge management system in six months, and it needs a way of explaining to its staff what knowledge management is.

- An environmental research facility flounders in its efforts to garner public attention because the scientific complexity of its work is hard for nonscientists to understand.

- A government agency restructures itself to support a new way of handling an intransigent community problem. The new approach is dramatically different, and the agency needs language that quickly and clearly conveys its essence.

In each instance, the organization develops a strategic message to help nonexperts grasp the significance of its work.

Building Identity and Understanding: Marketing Diabetes Research

In 1997, the Juvenile Diabetes Research Foundation International (then named the Juvenile Diabetes Foundation, or JDF) had a problem. It had completely restructured the way it awarded fifty million dollars annually for research intended to find the cause and cure for type 1 diabetes. The unique and innovative approach had taken twenty eminent scientists and management consultants a year to develop and had involved ninety other experts worldwide. However, few in the organization, except for its scientists, could explain why the changes were likely to hasten medical breakthroughs. Fundraisers stumbled when explaining it to donors. Press representatives stumbled when explaining it to the news media. Even management sometimes stumbled when explaining it to staff, chapter executives, and volunteers.

To meet this challenge, JDF created two different kinds of strategic messages. First, it created a message to explain the new approach in a manner that would build its institutional identity as innovative, a worthy investment for funders, and an organization that makes a difference in people's lives. Then, it created messages that described its key research goals in language that allowed those in various target audiences—from those living with diabetes who were anxious for a cure, to research scientists who were eager to answer significant medical questions—to clearly understand the research goals and why they were chosen.

This was the identity-building strategic message that explained the new approach: *Driven by the priorities of people with diabetes, JDF has restructured its research program along a business-world model in order to accelerate progress toward finding a cure for the disease and its complications.* In addition to the core message, it developed subset messages for its three target audiences: internal audiences (staff, volunteers, donors, referral sources), external audiences (funders, news media, Congress), and research audiences (researchers, medical institutions, medical foundations).

After developing the identity-building core message and its subsets, the organization created strategic messages that described each of its research goals. Each of the fifteen research goals was complex, highly technical, and difficult to explain. As a result, the messages ran long, but they provided an explanation of the foundation's most vital work to its three target audiences in ways that anyone could understand and in ways that spoke to each audience's specific desires.

(continued)

For example, the core message to describe the research goal of restoring normal blood sugar was this: *Next to finding a cure for diabetes, the biggest breakthrough in treating diabetes would be the ability to restore normal blood sugar levels. Efficient replacement of insulin would not "cure" diabetes because the autoimmune process would continue in the body. However, the dire consequences of sustained abnormal blood sugar levels might be lessened or eliminated.*

A Message Is Different from a Brand

Today's frequent use of the term brand leads many organizations to ask for help branding themselves when what they may really want is help with developing a strategic message. As noted above, a strategic message is developed in response to a wide range of needs, including clarifying institutional identity. It is this kind of strategic message that is often confused with branding.

An identity-focused strategic message and a brand are similar in some ways. Each is designed to make it easy for a person to recognize the organization quickly and to distinguish it clearly from other organizations. Each is changed rarely because its purpose is to build and sustain an identity for the organization, and that goal requires consistency over time. Both are created through strategic processes: they are tied to the larger mission and goals of the organization, they are aimed at specific groups and designed to appeal to the desires of those groups, and their development processes incorporate knowledge about external conditions including the brands and messages of competitors.

However, a brand and a strategic message differ in more ways than they are similar. Among the biggest differences are these:

- *Strategic messages and brands result in discrete products with completely different levels of flexibility and rigidity.* A strategic message uses only words, which may be delivered orally or in writing and can be adapted to the deliverer's style or situation while retaining the message's key points. The brand involves words and visuals that are fixed—logos, slogans, color schemes—and inviolate; once designed, these brand elements cannot be altered to accommodate individual style, medium, or occasion.

(Organizations that permit chapters or departments to tamper, for example, with the color of the logo, the typeface of the organization's name, or the organization's slogan cannot properly claim to be building a brand.)

Often an association or organization will request branding help when their true need is for a strategic message followed by a review of their graphic identity elements to ensure that the organization's visual identity is consistent with the strategic decisions made during the message development process. A local health agency whose corporate identity has evolved unplanned may develop a strategic message for its tenth anniversary so that stakeholders drawn to celebratory events glean a clearer understanding of the agency's mission and goals. A national nonprofit that acquires a new program may develop a strategic message to communicate how the new program furthers the organization's mission. It would be rare for an organization to initiate a full-fledged branding effort at these junctures. Rather than do that, most organizations should seek the benefits of a clear strategic message plus a review of graphic identity.

- *Strategic messages and brands are developed using different processes.* A strategic message can be developed in a few weeks. Those who will use the message are integrally involved in a structured process to produce it, often using an outside expert to facilitate the process and draft the message. Brand development is an extended process over weeks and months. It is primarily developed by branding companies and approved by organizational executives. Branding is a considerably more expensive process.

- *Strategic messages can be created without extensive market research.* Although it is very helpful (and a good idea) to conduct market research when drafting a strategic message, most associations and nonprofits lack the money to conduct formal market research, so it is rarely done. However, market research is essential to brand development, which is one reason branding takes longer and is more expensive.

A few examples make it easier to understand what a brand is and, therefore, how it differs from an identity-focused strategic message. The traditional definition of a brand is the *promise* that an organization makes to its customers, clients, and other audiences. In *The Brand Mindset,* Duane Knapp defines the brand promise as "the expected emotional and functional benefits of experiencing an organization's products and services, i.e., how an organization wants a customer to feel."[10]

We all understand commercial brands. When I bought a dishwasher recently, I chose a Whirlpool because experience led me to believe that it would meet my functional desire to have clean dishes and my emotional desire not to be frustrated. When my cousin buys a new BMW every two years, he does so because he wants a car that not only runs well but also projects an image of taste, expense, and class that makes him feel special.

The same thought processes and buyer responses apply to the products and services of nonprofit organizations and associations. They have brands, too, and they hope that people respond to them. For example,

- If I go to the Galápagos Islands with the National Geographic Society, I expect not only that I will have all my needs taken care of by an established, professionally run organization, but that I will experience the islands more fully—intellectually and emotionally—than if I went with a commercial travel company.

- If I go to the Art Institute of Chicago's web site to learn about Claude Monet, I believe I will get valid information that has been vetted by experts. If I simply want something approximating accuracy, there are 600,000 other places I can visit on the web to read about Monet rather than the Art Institute.

- When I donate twenty dollars to Heifer International, I believe that it will deliver a flock of chicks to a poor family to help them build or rebuild their life. I could send my twenty dollars to CARE or a hundred other organizations that provide a menu of services to help people around the world. In fact, when I give to disaster relief, I tend to give to CARE. However, when I want to help someone in an underdeveloped country live day-to-day, I tend to give to Heifer International. The experience that I associate with each organization is different because they are "branded" differently in my mind.

How do I develop these expectations? How do the National Geographic Society, the Art Institute of Chicago, and Heifer International make me feel that they will deliver what I believe they have promised? Part of it is direct experience with these organizations: tangible exposure through such things as publications, museum visits, and television programs. Part of it is reputation: what other people tell me about the organizations. Part of it is their visual representation: their web site, their brochures, and the variety of other ways they visually communicate that they are a professional, consistent, and capable organization. Part of it is what they say: they are informative, insightful, and caring. Part of it is coherence: what I hear and read about the organization is consistent with what programs and services it says it delivers and the values it espouses.

An organization creates a brand because it wishes to differentiate itself from other, especially similar, organizations as a means of facilitating interactions with all its target audiences. A professional society wants a member, upon seeing the society's brand, to instantly associate the society with certain attributes that will help retain that individual as a member. A cause-related organization wants a legislator, upon seeing the brand, to instantly associate the organization with attributes that will incline the legislator more favorably toward the organization's position on an issue. A human services agency wants a potential client, upon seeing the brand, to instantly associate the agency with attributes that will entice him to come in and be served.

An organization creates an identity-focused strategic message for the same reason that it creates a brand. There are several reasons why organizations opt for creating a strategic message and reviewing their corporate identity instead of undertaking a branding exercise: they want brand-like benefits more quickly and less expensively, they want to be involved in creating the product, or they desire a more flexible product.

A Message Is Different from a Frame

A strategic message is different from a *frame*, a word that, although newer than the term brand, is also increasingly popular in the lexicon of associations, nonprofits, and foundations. A frame, as defined by the Frameworks Institute, is "a small set of internalized concepts and values"[11] that, essentially, provide a "mental shortcut" to quickly assess new information.

Just as there is usually one situation that causes confusion between a strategic message and a brand—the need for institutional identity—there is usually one situation that causes confusion between a strategic message and a frame: the desire to persuade individuals to support a certain point of view related to politics or public policy.

A frame is virtually always created in connection with a political or public policy issue, and its goal is to get someone to see a concern or situation in a particular way even though it can be seen in a lot of different ways. We all know that something can be seen quite differently depending on the perspective. In the literal sense, we all have experience with perspective. If you are taking a picture of an individual, you may shoot a facial close-up, a vertical full-body picture, a horizontal picture of the individual in a group, or a wide-angle shot capturing the individual and the whole group with a vista of mountains and valley behind them—all the same scene, but seen in very different ways. We all have figurative experience with perspective as well, but we are less aware of it. Framing attempts to use specific words in a way that other possible perspectives are foreclosed, usually unconsciously. For example, linguist Deborah Tannen has pointed out that the use of the term "pro-choice" hampers those who support abortion rights because the word *choice* evokes a perspective—or a frame—that is consumeristic and thus implies inconsequentiality (like buying this or that swimsuit). On the other hand, "pro-life" advocates are strengthened by this term because the word *life* carries a moral frame with it; their position intuitively feels more correct because who can be against life?

The similarity between a strategic message and a frame is that both use words exclusively and both seek to leave the listener or reader with a point of view about a specific issue that arises partly from emotion and partly from intellect.

They are more different than they are similar, however. As noted earlier, a strategic message is used in a much wider variety of situations than a frame is, and to achieve a much greater range of goals. Achieving a particular political or cultural point of view is the goal of a frame, but it is only one of the uses of a strategic message. Strategic message development produces core and subset messages that have fully formed sentences, while a framing exercise produces a recommendation or set of recommendations about how to use specific words and references to talk about an issue or set of issues. A strategic message is created using a facilitated process involving a message development team from within the organization, whereas frame development is handled by outside consultants who study a variety of data to determine what frames may currently define an issue in the public mind before suggesting how to reframe the issue.

A frame is a powerful tool, and the knowledge gleaned from framing can increase the power of a strategic message. Message development can take the knowledge generated by framing experts and fold that thinking into the creation of the actual strategic message—giving the organization specific sentences that employ the desired frame.

A Message Is Different from a Slogan

A *slogan* is one element of a brand, the part that tries to capture the essence of an organization in a single catchy and evocative phrase, like the United Negro College Fund's "A mind is a terrible thing to waste." As such, it shares some of the brand's differences and similarities with strategic messages. A slogan is unchangeable and created almost always by outside experts, which differentiates it from a strategic message. Slogans share, with identity-focused strategic messages, the goal of helping create an institutional identity—helping a target audience more quickly and clearly distinguish an association or nonprofit from its competitors.

When a group gathers to create a strategic message, some people assume they are gathering to write a slogan. There is often palpable disappointment when it becomes clear that they are not going to toss around catchy phrases, witty expressions, or creative *bon mots*. Nonprofit professionals who would never consider getting out their colored pencils to create a logo are surprisingly ready to pull out their pens to write a slogan. Infrequently, a usable slogan may fall out of a message development process, but it is never the focus of the process.

Message and Slogan: Establishing "Lung Disease"

The late 1980s was a time of reflection and change at the American Lung Association (ALA). For more than eighty years, it had contributed significantly to removing tuberculosis from the list of fatal diseases and to convincing the public that smoking could kill you and harm others. Success with both issues had led the association to the place where it needed to find a new central focus for its work.

One focus that it considered was the panoply of ailments that could be, but had not yet been, clustered together in the public mind as lung disease. People knew heart disease and the American Heart Association. They knew cancer and the American Cancer Society. But they recognized asthma, chronic obstructive lung disease (COPD), lung cancer, and other illnesses individually rather than collectively as lung disease. The lack of clustering made it harder to promote lung health as a concept and the American Lung Association as an organization.

To help remedy the situation, the ALA created a core message and a new slogan for the organization. The difference between the two illustrates the difference between a strategic message and a slogan.

The purpose of the core message was to help create the concept of lung disease in the public mind and convey its seriousness. Success would mean an increased population of people who might support the association by taking action—volunteering, contributing, advocating, and so on. Created when the AIDS epidemic was first exploding, this is the core message that ALA adopted: *Lung disease is the third leading cause of death in America, and the death rate is growing faster than for almost any other major disease except AIDS. We need your help now to fight lung disease.*

At the same time, the ALA adopted a new slogan to replace the one that it had used for many years. The slogan was also designed to create the concept of lung disease. However, it was not expected to activate. It was intended to make people associate the American Lung Association with more diseases that they might have before. The new slogan was: *When you can't breathe, nothing else matters.*

A Message Is Different from an Elevator Speech

To some, a strategic message looks like an *elevator speech*—the language we are expected to have ready for the imaginary moment when someone riding with us on an elevator asks what we do. As with brands, frames, and slogans, there are similarities between strategic messages and elevator speeches as well as differences.

They resemble each other in three ways. Both have multiple parts, a "quick catch" component that snares a listener's attention and then follows immediately with information designed to connect to that person's interests. Each is flexible in its language; the person delivering either is encouraged to use language that feels personally comfortable and appropriate to the situation and target listener. Finally, both are ore often created by internal message development teams rather than outside creative agencies.

However, there are also differences between a strategic message and an elevator speech. First, most elevator speeches are developed to respond to some version of the question, who are you? Second, elevator speeches are always spoken, while strategic messages are used in a variety of written, as well as oral, communications. The most significant difference between the two, however, is that strategic messages are designed to be used by people with varying levels of communication ability, whereas elevator speeches, in truth, require significant communication skill. An effective elevator speech is interactive and requires the ability to pick up a conversational clue about a stranger's desires and quickly respond with a relevant comment that lays a foundation for further exchange. Such dexterity demands a high level of communication skill. Few people in an organization possess that level of communication dexterity, yet many people are frequently called on to connect in a quick and compelling manner with people who are important to the organization. One of the advantages of a strategic message is that such people are supported with set language that is simple and effective and that they can fall back on if they choose not to use their own words.

Summary

- A strategic message is a set of statements that prompts one or more targeted audiences to take a desired action.

- A strategic message consists of a core statement that is heard by all audiences and subset statements that are specific to each individual target audience.

- A strategic message does three things: it captures the attention of a target audience, it focuses the subsequent conversation on attaining mutual desires, and it results in action you and your listener both want.

- There are three common reasons why strategic messages are developed: to prompt an action, to create an institutional identity, and to describe a complex idea or program.

- A strategic message is different from a brand, a frame, a slogan, and an elevator speech, although it shares some attributes of each.

Discussion Questions

1. Can everyone in our organization explain what we do clearly, simply, and in a way that connects with our stakeholders?

2. We've been talking about needing to "brand" the organization, but is that what we really mean? Or is our need simply a better way of saying what we do? Or do we really just want to look at our logo and see if it needs to be changed?

3. Are we so focused on individual audiences that we don't deliver an overarching core message that reaches stakeholders as they move between audiences?

4. Should we go one step further with our framing work and use that knowledge to help us develop a strategic message that we can all use?

5. An elevator speech would be helpful, but can all of us think quickly enough on our feet to use it? Do most of us need actual words that we can fall back on?

3. The Core Principles of Strategic Messages

THE BASIC PRINCIPLES that underlie strategic messaging are easy, and you may already know them intuitively.

Like objects that are hidden in plain sight, the fundamentals of strategic message development are common truths that are played out in the words and actions of people every day.

That doesn't mean developing a strategic message is easy to do. We all know that things can be easy to grasp and hard to execute. Ask any golfer, or any chef, or any spouse. But how you develop a strategic message is for future chapters. This chapter focuses on what you need to think about as you embark on messaging.

Action Drives Message

Begin with the end in mind, as author Stephen Covey says.[12] The first key to strategic message development is knowing what you want to occur as a result of your message.

This concept of beginning with the end in mind is almost absurdly obvious. If you leave Indianapolis on a five-day road trip, you might end up in Playa del Carmen, Mexico, or Vancouver, Canada, or Denver, Colorado—but if you needed to be in San Francisco, you would not necessarily have gotten there unless you had decided on that destination and driven toward it. We all realize that an association, foundation, or nonprofit needs to know where it wants to go if it expects to get there.

However obvious the concept, identifying the end—the action you want your audience to take—is often overlooked by message developers. Many, if not most, strategic message development groups start with the assumption that everyone in the group knows what action is sought by developing a message. This assumption is almost always wrong. Just as strategic planning must start with a decision to affirm or change the organizational mission, strategic message development must start with a decision about what action the organization seeks to effect through messaging.

Groups often become restive when pushed to articulate the action. They are more comfortable brainstorming words and phrases or discussing which stakeholder groups are most important to reach. They'll digress into a conversation about the web site or the need for more news media attention. Again, this mirrors strategic planning because planning committees often want to talk about specific programs or goals before ensuring there is agreement about mission. In both strategic messaging and strategic planning, reluctance usually flows from the fact that most people are more comfortable discussing smaller tactical issues than larger strategic ones. In most instances, identifying the action focus for the message is a significant strategic issue.

Articulating the action goal of a strategic message is the hardest part of the development process for most groups. Being precise about what their organization wants to accomplish is not, unfortunately, a strength of some nonprofits. However, it is an essential ingredient in strategic message development.

Self-Interest Drives Action

The second key concept is as obvious as the first: *people act because they want something.* Their self-interest moves them to take action. The reality that self-interest drives both attention and action is difficult for many in the voluntary sector to acknowledge; it is usually less of a problem for professional associations because they exist to meet the interests of members, and they operate accordingly.

A successful strategic message is almost impossible to develop without accepting the fact that target audiences will respond based on their own interests, not yours. Without this orientation, nonprofits inevitably end up telling their constituents what to do or think, which is rarely a recipe for success. Successful messages speak to the self-interest of the audience in some manner.

The self-interest that people seek to satisfy may be tangible or intangible. It may be a feeling: *I feel generous when I donate to the United Way. I feel like I am doing my civic duty when I help register voters.* It may be a material benefit: *Maintaining my association membership will give me access to the latest developments in my profession. Joining the society will allow me to get discounts on their trips.* It may be an anticipated benefit: *Being part of the coalition will bring the organization greater visibility. I'll volunteer to work on Saturday to finish the report because it will show my dedication and increase my chances of getting the director's job.* Or the action may actually be inaction: *I've got to quit disagreeing with the board president on the small stuff if we're going to work together this year. We've got to stop requiring older volunteers to work nights if we want to keep them working with us.*

When the staff and boards of charitable, human service, and cause-related organizations resist the importance of self-interest, it is usually because they believe people should do good for the sake of doing good, not to get something in return. Although this attitude is less prevalent than it was some years ago, it is still frequently heard. The attitude presupposes, detrimentally, that self-interest is by definition ungenerous.

Self-interest is not, by nature, ungenerous. It is, by nature, simply natural. We pay attention to what is more interesting to us rather than less interesting. It hardly indicates a lack of generosity if an environmentalist wants to work for the Wilderness Society instead of Head Start or if a civil rights expert would rather serve on the board of the Massachusetts NAACP than the Boston Symphony.

Self-interest is not inherently a character flaw. However, being unwilling to accept its importance as a motivator will fatally flaw message development.

Self-interest is not inherently a character flaw. Being unwilling to accept its importance as a motivator, however, will fatally flaw message development.

Desire Trumps Need

Peter Brinkerhoff says it best in his book *Mission-Based Marketing:* "People *have* needs. People *seek* wants."[13] When identifying an audience's self-interest, it is important to focus more on what the audience wants than on what it needs.

Most associations, nonprofits, and foundations are focused on need. Social service agencies concentrate on meeting clients' needs for food, shelter, health care, and a plethora of other necessities of life. Professional associations seek to serve members' requirements for the latest trade information, cutting-edge professional practices, and links to others in the field. Cause-related organizations strive to fulfill activists' demand for timely information, organized action, and effective tools.

This focus on what stakeholders need contributes to the tendency of non-profit groups to *tell* their stakeholders what they should do rather than *ask* them what they want. Groups believe that their organization is being relied on to provide what members need and, as the experts in their field, the organization staff can best decide what programs should be delivered. The "I know what you need" culture is pervasive—if not predominant—in the nonprofit, foundation, and association communities. And it is a major impediment to successful message development.

Once we think about it, personal experience has taught most of us how driven people are by desire instead of need. I need spinach, but I desire chocolate—which do I reach for more often? I need to talk to my boss about taking next Friday off to travel to the family reunion, but I don't want to endure another of his temper flare-ups—how long do I delay? I believe that the country needs to address important environmental issues, but an SUV makes me feel like no one can mess with me—what do I buy?

Even when human conditions appear to be situations of obvious need, action may be driven equally—or more—by desire. We *need* to eat to stay alive, but, with no disrespect to Abraham Maslow's hierarchy of needs, we eat because we *want* to live. Children *need* to be supervised, but some parents *want* to have fun, so they "just run down the street" to a party, telling themselves their kids will be okay even without a babysitter. Through painful experience, people with various mental illnesses know they *need* to stay on medication or face serious consequences, but many stop taking their pills because they *want* to feel "normal."

The Illinois Department of Transportation proved the power of desire in 2000 when it began replacing the didactic "Give 'Em a Brake" signs at highway construction sites with evocative signs that said "My Daddy/Mommy Works Here—Slow Down Please." In the first year, the state had a 30 percent reduction in work zone fatalities.[14]

Common Desire Is the Secret of Success

A very simple diagram captures both the concept and process that's at the heart of strategic message development. This diagram—which I call the Action Connection—shows where the desire of the organization overlaps with the desire of its target audience. The diagram consists of two circles illustrating organization desire and audience desire. If the circles overlap, there is there is shared desire, which is the foundation for continued communication. It is from this shared desire that action originates.

The Action Connection

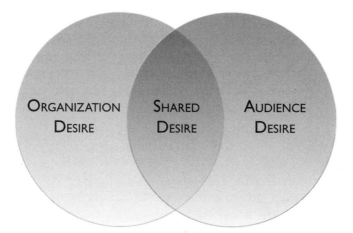

ORGANIZATION DESIRE   SHARED DESIRE   AUDIENCE DESIRE

Admittedly, it is possible to capture someone's attention momentarily in the absence of shared desire. Each of us has been captivated by a clever thirty-second commercial for a product we will never consider buying. We may even have been captured a few times by the same commercial. However, we are caught but not held: once we've had our chuckle, we are done paying attention. What attracts us is the joy of being entertained. The desire of the company—that we buy its product—will not be satisfied. Our attention is like cotton candy, there is a quick sweet moment that disappears in an instant.

A quick sweet moment is not the goal of a strategic message. Keeping the attention of the target audience so that they can be moved to "buy the product" is the goal. In the case of associations, nonprofits, and foundations, the product may be a conference or book, but more commonly the product is an action like joining the association, donating blood, feeding the hungry, sending money, volunteering, participating in or purchasing the service provided, changing behavior, or voting for highway bonds.

If no overlap can be created, then no effective message can be designed because the essential ingredient for sustained communication—shared desire—is absent.

There comes a point in strategic message development when the Action Connection is either recognizable or obviously absent. If no overlap can be created, then no effective message can be designed because the essential ingredient for sustained communication, shared desire, is absent. A sound bite may be created—a cleverly worded phrase or two that makes the message team feel creative—but it will not be any more effective as a message than the entertaining thirty-second commercial. It will not capture the audience's attention and hold it so that more information can be conveyed, which is what an effective message does.

Without the shared interest that is reflected visually in the Action Connection diagram, there is no basis for continued connection, which is the foundation for moving people to action.

Less Is More

The problem with nonprofit messaging is that too many organizations "want to have four goals, ten audiences, and twenty messages," notes Dana Shelley, director of strategic communications for the Annie E. Casey Foundation.[15] This is a sure recipe for failure.

Fewer words, fewer audiences, and fewer major points result in the strategic message being more easily remembered both by the individuals who deliver it and the individuals who hear it. More often than not, there is an inverse relationship between the impact of a message and its number of words, message points, and audiences: there is higher impact with fewer factors.

There are various estimates of how long people pay attention to what they hear and see before they decide whether to engage more fully or think about something else. They spend less time making a decision about a web page than a newsletter. They tune out faster if they have never heard of the speaker than if the speaker is a celebrity they like. But all these estimates share one consistency: the time spans are all expressed in seconds.

When speaking, a person may have fifteen to twenty seconds to catch someone's ear, which is why a good core message is rarely longer than twenty-five to thirty words. If one is initially successful, one may have upwards of a minute to capture a listener's attention, which is why there are usually no more than three subset messages.

Think of messaging like fishing. A message is bait: If the bait is too big, the fish may nibble but swim away. If the bait is the right size, the fish takes it in and you have greatly increased your chance of hooking the fish. And, once hooked, you have time to reel the fish in. Similarly, if the message is the right length and hooks the listener, you have time to use subset messages and, ultimately, speak at some length about your concern.

A longer message not only fails to connect as powerfully with an audience as a shorter one does, it is also hard for staff, board members, and volunteers to remember. As a result, the speaker may falter in delivering the message and erode the listener's confidence in the speaker and the message itself. The person delivering the message is also more likely to leave out an important aspect of the strategic message because there is simply too much to recall. Worst of all, staff, volunteers, or board members may simply choose not to use the message because the speaker doesn't want to either stammer in delivering it or fail to "do it right" by remembering all the message points. A message, no matter how artfully crafted, is worthless if it is not delivered.

The most successful strategic messages contain no more than three major points. The speaker usually cannot remember more than three, and the listener cannot successfully process more than three.

The most successful strategic messages contain no more than three major points. Fewer than three is fine, more than three is not. Again, the speaker usually cannot remember more than three, and the listener cannot successfully process more than three. Personal experience teaches us that three is a natural maximum. The rule of three appears often in our speaking and reading: think of the Declaration of Independence's "life, liberty, and the pursuit of happiness" or the fire-safety rule "stop, drop, and roll."

A graphic from *How to Be Prepared to Think on Your Feet*[16] illustrates precisely why three is a stopping point. We may be able to remember seven items on a grocery store list, but our mental ability to process *interrelated* information stops at three. One piece of information can be processed, well, one way. Two pieces of information can be processed two different ways. Three pieces of information can be processed six different ways, which is a strain. But four pieces of information can be processed *twenty-four* different ways. That is simply too much for the mind.

Processing Information

Two pieces of information can be processed, or related, two ways:

A–B   B–A

Three pieces of information can be processed, or related, in six different ways:

A–BC   B–AC   C–AB   A–CB   B–CA   C–BA

Four pieces of information can be processed, or related, in twenty-four different ways:

A–BCD	B–ACD	C–ABD	D–ABC
A–BDC	B–ADC	C–ADB	D–ACB
A–CBD	B–CAD	C–BAD	D–BAC
A–CDB	B–CDA	C–BDA	D–BCA
A–DBC	B–DAC	C–DAB	D–CAB
A–DCB	B–DCA	C–DBA	D–CBA

From *How to Be Prepared to Think on Your Feet* by Stephen C. Rafe. Copyright © 1990 by Stephen C. Rafe. Reprinted by permission of HarperCollins Publishers.

Summary

Five concepts (the first four of which are summed up in the diagram titled the Action Connection, page 35) are integral to effective strategic message development. They are

- Action drives message—know *why* you speak.

- Self-interest drives action—to move people, speak to their self-interest, not yours.

- Desire trumps need—people have needs; people seek wants.

- No common desire means no message—without overlap between your organization's desire and your audience's desire, an effective strategic message is impossible.

- Less is more—fewer words, fewer audiences, fewer points equals more success.

Discussion Questions

1. When we talk, do we talk with the end in mind? Do we all agree on what that end is?

2. Can we accept that people take action because they want something, or are we uncomfortable thinking that way?

3. Are we reluctant to appeal to what our audiences desire? Do we feel there is something wrong with doing that?

4. If the concept that audiences seek what they desire is new to us, in what ways might our programs and messages change if we embrace this concept?

5. As we try to deliver what our stakeholders want, are we careful to make sure that we get what we want too?

4. *Step One*
Identify the Action Desired

ORGANIZATIONS COMMUNICATE for a reason. What is yours?

Few children haven't heard an angry parent scold: "Think before you speak!" We said to our best friend that her new haircut was funny-looking. We told the neighborhood that our parents thought the couple next door might get a divorce. We let slip to our grandmother that pot was found in our cousin's locker at high school. What were you thinking when you said that—or were you thinking?

Organizations can be similarly admonished. Many of them fail to think before they speak. As a result, they say things they wish they hadn't or don't say things they wish they had.

Creating a strategic message is a five-step process that begins by articulating what the organization wants to occur as a result of communicating with others. As noted in the last chapter, the first principle of strategic messaging is that action drives message, and the first step in developing a strategic message is deciding what action is sought. Does the association want the federal government to revise regulations certifying organic foods? Does the foundation want its grantees to initiate annual board evaluations? Does the city choral arts society want volunteers to identify potential donors among their friends?

Identifying the action that the organization desires is usually the most difficult part of strategic message development. One reason organizations fail to identify their message goal is that they can't decide what they actually want to have happen. Another reason is that internal politics make it uncomfortable to articulate what the organization really wants to accomplish. A third reason is that leadership has delegated strategic message development to a single department—usually communications—rather than involving an interdisciplinary team in the creative process.

Messaging Starts by Choosing the Desired Action

When an organization knows what it wants, the result can be powerful. Mothers whose children were killed by drunk drivers founded Mothers Against Drunk Driving (MADD) in 1980, when drinking and driving was barely recognized as a social problem. The original name was Mothers Against Drunk *Drivers,* and it focused on getting drunk drivers off the road by putting them in jail. Within a couple years, however, MADD leaders realized that they wanted to stop the problem before it started; the action the group wanted was for people to abstain from driving when they had been drinking. They focused on that action and joined others in popularizing the concept of having a designated driver—which has become a household term, a widespread practice, and a powerful influence in helping lower the incidence of drunk driving nationwide.

Those working for an organization are often unaware, until they start strategic message development, that they do not share a common opinion about what action they seek. Consider the example of a community organization that is dedicated to lowering the number of traffic accidents caused by drivers using cell phones. It is one of ten organizations invited to testify before the city council regarding the problem. What action does the organization want the city council to take? Part of the group wants the council to ban cell phone use by drivers. Others want a public campaign to educate drivers that cell phone use causes accidents, especially for drivers over age fifty. Others want to promote the concept of "park 'n phone." These actions are all consistent with the organization's mission, but offering all three to the council will probably ensure that council members will not recall, after listening to nine other speakers, what the organization advocated and may reduce the chance that any action is legislated.

The purpose of strategic message development is *to put the right information into the hands of the right people to prompt the action the organization desires.* When an organization or association knows what it wants to accomplish, it is much easier to figure out who needs to be activated to achieve the goal and what they need to hear to act. When an organization does not know, it often ends up talking to people who are unable to effect the change it seeks—or talking to the right people but about the wrong things.

The purpose of strategic message development is to put the right information into the hands of the right people to prompt the action the organization desires.

Putting the right information into the hands of the right people to prompt the action you desire is not only the purpose of message development, it also suggests the process for creating a strategic message. The process works backwards from the end of the phrase.

Step one. The first step in developing a strategic message is to determine what action the organization is trying to bring about. All of the strategic message development process flows from the organization's clear identification of the action it seeks to achieve.

Step two. Once the action has been decided, the organization turns to identifying who can make that action occur. Those who can effect the action are the right people or, in marketing terms, the target audiences for the message.

Step three. After the audiences are identified, the next step is to determine why those people would want to take the action that the organization desires. In other words, what's in it for them? Understanding their motivation and speaking to it is delivering the right information because it is the information most likely to move them to action.

Step four. Next, the organization must determine the overlap between what it wants and what the target audiences want. Think of the Action Connection diagram: where the two circles overlap is the area of common desire—where the message needs to exist. If no overlap can be found, no effective strategic message can be created. This step usually occurs quickly, as the overlap (or disconnect) is usually apparent by the end of step three.

Step five. Once the overlap has been identified, the last step is deciding how the message will be communicated to the target audiences—the words that will put the message into their heads. If an organization is not clear about the action it seeks, it cannot accurately name the actors or create language that connects with their desires and compels them to act.

The entire strategic message development process is captured in the Action Connection diagram. Internalize the visual, and you have most of the major principles and all the steps of the process.

The Action Connection and Message Development Steps

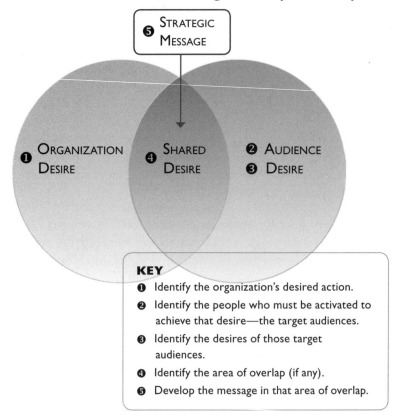

KEY

❶ Identify the organization's desired action.
❷ Identify the people who must be activated to achieve that desire—the target audiences.
❸ Identify the desires of those target audiences.
❹ Identify the area of overlap (if any).
❺ Develop the message in that area of overlap.

Awareness Is Rarely Action

If nonprofit organizations were computer programs, their default action for strategic message development would be to "create awareness." An association of professional accountants wants members to *be aware* of its best practices program. A Special Olympics chapter wants professionals who treat people with special needs to be aware of the competitions. A children's museum wants teachers to be aware of its exceptional programs.

Is that really what they want? What good is it if accountants are aware of best practices but ignore them? If occupational and physical therapists know about the Special Olympics but never encourage their patients to join the games? If teachers recognize the potential benefits of the children's museum but never use any of them?

Obviously, awareness is not what these organizations really want. The association wants accountants not just to know about the best practices program but to use it. The association hopes that, by using its program, accountants improve their services and deliver more value to society *and* experience the value of membership and are thus more likely to renew. Medical professionals must persuade their special-needs patients to compete in the local Special Olympics so the chapter can achieve its goal of providing athletic training and competition. And teachers must bring their classes to the museum or employ museum resources in the classroom before the museum can have the opportunity to educate students.

Similarly, some organizations will say that the goal of their strategic message is to *inform* or to *persuade*. These may, indeed, be steps that must be taken to activate a target audience or parts of the audience. However, they make poor endpoints for a strategic message for the same reason that *awareness* is a poor endpoint. One wonders how much less successful MADD would have been in reducing the number of drunk drivers on the road if its goal had been merely to make people aware or persuade them that drunk driving was a problem, rather than put an end to drunk driving.

There is nothing wrong with an organization beginning the strategic message development process by saying that the action it desires is to create awareness or to inform. There is a lot wrong with it *staying* there, in most instances.

The Awareness Exception

There is one exception to the rule that awareness is not an acceptable action. There are times when a strategic message is created to help increase institutional identity or describe a difficult topic. Here, the message is developed primarily to create awareness, to position an organization in a target audience's mind so that future communications will be more easily heard and future attempts to activate audiences will be more successful. This is not always the case with such messages, but it can be.

In the late 1990s, when the Juvenile Diabetes Research Foundation International developed a strategic message to describe each of its research goals, it did so to provide various professionals in the organization with a tool for explaining, specifically, what the organization was trying to discover about type 1 diabetes and why knowing that particular information would significantly advance the fight against the disease and its complications. The intent was not to spark a singular action, but to provide language and understanding that would make it easier for a fundraiser to solicit a donor, for communications staff to approach reporters, or for a staff scientist to talk to a prospective researcher.

When the Knight Journalism Initiative was launched in 2003, the project director wanted potential target audiences to understand immediately how the initiative differed from a plethora of other programs aimed at changing the way news is reported in the United States. The strategic message was intended to position the new project clearly so that target audiences would be more receptive to being approached later when programmatic operations got up and running. It did that. (The process also helped the director shape the programmatic offerings and create a name that conveyed the mission rather than simply serving as a label. The framework used to develop a strategic message can be used to achieve other organizational goals, as will be seen in Chapter 11.)

It is important to note that the process for developing a strategic message is the same even when the identified action is merely awareness. The organization still must identify target audiences—those it wants to make aware— because it will later try to activate them in some way. The organization must still understand what audience desire is being met by knowing what the organization is doing. And it still must express the message in such a way that target audiences hear some desire of theirs is being met.

Messaging Is Strategic, Not Tactical

Too often, organizations view developing a message as a tactic, like issuing a press release or sending out an activist alert. Whip up a snappy sentence or two and, voilá, we have a message. Wrong. You have a snappy sentence, maybe even a quotable quote—a useful, tactical tool—but you do not have a *strategic* message.

Message development is a strategic function because it involves the totality of an organization. It involves mission: is the action that we wish to effect one that is consistent with our mission? It involves programs: is the action that we wish to achieve one that aligns with the programs we deliver and, thus, can we support or extend the action we are urging others to take? It involves communications: can we reach the audiences we need to activate? It involves planning and resource allocation: if we cannot currently support an action that we have identified as being critically important or reach an audience that we must reach, can we develop the capacities we need and, if so, how long will it take and what resources will be needed?

When an organization develops a strategic message for the purpose of strengthening its institutional identity, it frequently engages in discussions that sound very much like those that occur when an organization writes its mission statement. As noted in Chapter 2, however, there is an important difference between a strategic message and a mission statement. The mission statement is written from the perspective of the organization and has two purposes: first, to state why the organization is in business and, second, to help it make decisions about how to allocate its time, money, and personnel to achieve its goals. A strategic message is worded from the perspective of the target audience and has one purpose: to persuade that audience to take action consistent with the organization's desire.

In order to create an identity-focused strategic message, a group must have a clear understanding and articulation of its mission. Most high-functioning enterprises have mission statements that have been carefully created.

Increasingly, however, even high-functioning enterprises have mission statements that have not been discussed for several years. The speed with which the world is moving has led many organizations to shorten or postpone traditional strategic planning, which is the process that usually provides the opportunity to revisit, discuss, and possibly revise the organizational mission. Pent-up need for such conversation may lead to it happening in the course of strategic message development.

On the other hand, strategic message development sometimes prompts the creation of an organization's first mission statement, especially if the entity is smaller, like a single program or an organization that is just moving from the stage of experimental program to permanent institution. Clarity of mission is so essential to effective strategic message development that, if none exists, it needs to be created. Although the message development process may not need to stop while a mission statement is formally adopted, there does need to be a full discussion and the achievement of clear direction.

Message Development Is Not Just for Communicators

As a strategic function that cuts across departmental concerns, strategic message development should not be solely the responsibility of the communications department. One reason is that the action that the communications department identifies as being the message driver may be too narrow. A cross-functional team is much more likely to identify an action goal that is broad enough to serve the interests of all departments that will relying on the message to move their constituencies.

Strategic messages created only by the communications staff do not achieve the success of those created by a cross-functional team for three additional reasons. First, others in the organization have not helped develop it, so they are much less likely to use it. Second, all aspects of strategic message development—the action, the target audiences, and the audiences' desires—have been seen from only a communications perspective, not from a multidisciplinary approach that usually provides greater clarity, understanding, and success. Third, the choice of words in the message may sound good to the

The Mission-Message Link

In 2003, a large national foundation transferred management of a five-year-old, multi-million-dollar project called the State Government Management Initiative (SGMI)[17] from one grantee to another. SGMI provided policy information and management data to state governments. The new administering entity wanted a message that clearly articulated the initiative's purpose to the nationwide network of academics, state government employees, elected officials, and other professionals who were integrally involved in the initiative's work and whose involvement determined its success. The first step in the strategic message development process was to identify the action that the group wanted to have happen—basically, a reflection of the project's mission. However, the initiative's mission had never been articulated.

Before a strategic message could be developed, the mission needed to be stated. In preparation for the first message development meeting, members of the message development team—composed of all the project leaders—were asked to write down the initiative's mission. In a scene familiar to nonprofit veterans, the preparatory exercise revealed that, although half of the message development group had been working on the project since its inception, there was disagreement about what precisely the initiative was trying to accomplish. Some thought that the project was intended to enhance management capacity. Some thought it was supposed improve policy development and increase state governments' effectiveness. Some thought it was to improve life for state residents.

In the end, a working mission statement was developed so that discussion could proceed and the group could identify the desired action. The working statement expressed the mission as *to improve the performance of state government in meeting the demands placed on them by the political process.* The mission discussion provided the foundation for the group's decision about the action that it desired: SGMI wanted the data and analysis it provided to be "sticky." In other words, it wanted its quality, dissemination, and accessibility to be such that policymakers and government administrators would return to the data and analysis and use them whenever they addressed related management issues. Identifying that action drove not only the message development process, but also decisions related to resource allocation, communication strategy, and evaluation.

In the end, the group adopted a core message reflective of audience desires that read: *SGMI gives state governments information they can use to improve their management and achieve their goals.*

communications staff, but others in the organization may see words in the message that will elicit negative responses from some audiences.

Although professional communicators are often the first to recognize the need for a strategic message, a cross-functional team that includes the highest levels of an organization must be involved in developing one. In small- and medium-sized organizations, the chief executive officer is usually involved; in very large organizations, one or more senior vice presidents are. Very often, one or more members of the board of directors serve on the message development team.

Choosing the Action Can Cause Conflict

Unresolved organizational politics can kill effective message development, and such politics are most likely to surface as the organization chooses the action it desires. The reason so many organizations identify awareness as their desired action is that awareness is an easy goal for everyone to agree on. It does not create friction between programs, each of which may want its service to be the foremost message goal. It sidesteps disagreements between board members committed to radical change and staff members who labor daily to make incremental change. Not everyone may agree on what action the organization should advocate, but they can all agree that greater awareness of the problem would be helpful.

An easy agreement should be a signal that nothing significant has been decided. Tough strategic decisions are seldom made easily. And deciding precisely what action the organization wants to elicit is a tough strategic decision. It is, as mentioned earlier, the hardest decision that the message development group will make in the entire process.

As part of the message development process, the group should write down what action the strategic message will be designed to elicit. It is a mistake to assume—because everyone was present for the action discussion and decision—that everyone agrees on what the decision was. Anyone who has served on a few strategic planning committees knows that the first step in such planning is to ensure that everyone is on the same page regarding the mission. The same holds true with strategic messaging committees—make sure everyone is focused on the same action. The best way to do that is to articulate and write down the action sought.

Groups sometimes resist spending time on articulating the action. They press to get on with the process. One helpful way to demonstrate the need for spending this time is to request that each member of the message development team bring to the first meeting a written statement of the action that will be the focus of the message. Simply going around the room and having people read their statements often convinces the group that they may be starting from very different places and need to reconcile the differences.

Discussions about action can help the organization realize that it wants a bigger action than it usually talks about. For example,

> Staff of a new program to introduce mid-career training for journalists—a profession notoriously resistant to staff development—realized that they did not simply wish to train professionals, but they also wanted to reframe how the profession viewed training. The program's strategic message was *to make staff development as much a part of journalism as deadlines are.*

> Staff of a regional program that placed young people on the boards of directors of local service agencies realized that they wanted to do more than simply train young people for board service; they wanted to help youths and adults develop mutual relationships that resulted in changed attitudes toward each other. The strategic message said that the organization *helps young people and adults think differently about each other so that they can work together to change society.*

The difficulty of resolving often passionately held opinions about the targeted action is one reason why an outside facilitator can be instrumental to the success of the development process. It doesn't matter whether an organization engages a paid facilitator or taps a volunteer. What matters is that the facilitator is experienced and firm enough to force the group to make a clear decision about the action it seeks.

Summary

- Action drives message development.

- The purpose of strategic messaging is *to put the right information into the hands of the right people to prompt the action you desire.*

- The process of strategic message development works backwards in the phrase above; begin with the end (the action) in mind.

- Awareness is rarely an acceptable action.

- A strategic message *is* strategic, not tactical; it involves the totality of the organization.

- Choosing an action may require revisiting or even creating an organizational or program mission.

Discussion Questions

1. When we speak or write, do we know what action we actually want to prompt?

2. Do we resist articulating the action we want because we are afraid we cannot get consensus about the action?

3. Are we so focused on making people aware of a problem that we forget to tell them what to do about it?

4. Is the action we seek something that advances our mission? Is it an action we can support through our program, communications, or other operations? If not, is it important enough to make changes so that we can support the action?

5. Are we willing to involve a cross-disciplinary team, including senior leaders, in the development of our strategic message?

5. *Step Two*
Identify the Target Audiences

YOU KNOW WHAT ACTION you want to effect. Who can make that happen?

After a group has finished the heavy lifting of deciding what action it seeks to achieve, it turns in step two to a question that is usually easier to answer: *Who must act to achieve our goal?* Whoever must act is the person or people you need to reach, the ones at whom you must aim, or target, your message. Not surprisingly, they are called your target audiences.

Most of us know the term *target market* from the commercial world. Manufacturers want to reach and activate target markets because the people in those clusters are most likely to purchase their products: Tide detergent targets women because they are the people in the family who usually buy the detergent. Craftsman tools target men because they buy more power saws than women. Ballistic Skateboard Company targets teenage boys because who the heck else would risk their necks on those things?

The same concept applies to the target audiences of foundations, associations, and nonprofits. Organizations target people who can take the action they seek. The membership department of the American Medical Association targets doctors because they pay the association membership dues. The public policy arm of the Chesapeake Bay Foundation targets Maryland legislators because they decide whether power plants in the state will have to reduce pollution-causing emissions.

Sometimes, companies target people who do not make the purchase decision themselves but determine what purchase is made. For example, Froot Loops cereal's marketers target young children not because they expect your three-year-old to whip out cash at the checkout, but because they expect his incessant pleading will result in your purchase of the cereal. Similarly, nonprofits may target people who do not directly take the desired action but whose influence may determine what action occurs.

Identifying the target audiences for the strategic message is easier than articulating the action desired, but it is still an issue that bears careful consideration. Audience selection usually implies at least some anticipation of the outreach strategy that the organization will develop in pursuit of its goal. Therefore, in selecting audiences, organizations need to consider what their current capacity is to reach those audiences or what capacities they are willing to develop.

Target Audiences Come in All Sizes

Target audiences can be of any size except one: unlimited. There is no target audience named "everyone." One person can be the sole target audience for a strategic message if the action of that one person can achieve the result that an organization seeks. Or the target audience may have thousands in it. Many times, a message will be targeted simultaneously at some audiences that are quite small and others that are quite large.

A smaller audience may be advantageous because it may be possible to speak to fewer people's desires more specifically. In addition, a smaller audience may mean communication vehicles can be chosen that would otherwise be prohibitive because of cost or some other factor. However, size itself should not be a key factor in choosing target audiences. The key question is, How large must the audience be to achieve the action sought?

Despite the assertion of some in the nonprofit world, there can be no target audience named "the public." It may be true that everyone should care about your particular issue, but is it true that everyone cares enough to take action? Without question, everyone should care about global warming, children dying of AIDS in Africa, older Americans who lack health insurance

Target Audiences Versus Target Market

Many forward-thinking associations, foundations, and nonprofits now use the term *target markets* instead of *target audiences*. The change is a good one. I encourage its use, which is why I use it in the book title. Unfortunately, most in the field are loathe to use the term because of the commercial connotations of the word "market." For that reason I mostly use the term target audience in this book; I do not want my readers to miss my larger message because they react adversely to one word. Although this book uses the term target audience, I encourage use of the term target market because it keeps message developers focused on the action they are trying to effect. The goal of strategic message development is to move groups to take action; the term "market" implies customers—people who are in action—but the term "audience" implies people who are listening without necessarily acting. Having a goal of listening is tantamount to having a goal of awareness, not action.

and cannot afford needed medicines, wars across the globe, bigotry and discrimination of every kind, urban sprawl, and a hundred other worthy worries. But who has time to do anything about any one of these, much less all of them?

> **The stubborn insistence that "the public" be a target audience virtually guarantees that the strategic message will fail to achieve its purpose.**

The stubborn insistence that "the public" be a target audience virtually guarantees that the strategic message will fail to achieve its purpose. Even if "the public" is only one of the audiences, it will destroy the message's effectiveness as developers strain to construct a core message that overarches the desires of *everyone*. Who can even name a truly universal desire, given the dramatic differences people see in life? You might once have been safe saying, for example, that world peace is a universal desire, but that assertion could be strongly challenged by some today.

Any strategic message that attempts to connect with everyone will, in truth, rarely connect with anyone. Talking to everyone usually results in being heard by no one.

Target Audiences Can Change

Target audiences can change in the course of achieving an objective. As the people who need to act change, so do the audiences and the strategic messages they receive. In one phase, an organization may need to talk to audiences A, B, and C to get from the first point in a process to the second. Having achieved the second point and wanting to reach the third, it may no longer need to talk to audience A, but it may need now to talk to a new group, audience D. Many aspects of the strategic message may stay the same, such as most of the core message, but a new group of subset messages needs to be created for audience D to ensure that it hears its desires are being met.

This was the case with the Center for the Study of Social Policy (CSSP), whose messaging experience is reported at length in Chapter 10. CSSP had developed a radical new approach to preventing child abuse and neglect that was based not in the legal system, as is traditionally the case, but in the early childhood care system. It was ready to move the idea from the conceptual stage to the testing stage, and to do that it needed to work with large fields of professionals—child abuse and prevention specialists, early childhood practitioners, and government social service agencies. Its strategy for activating those fields was first to engage key leaders in each field. Once those leaders were supportive of the approach, CSSP revised its strategic message to approach frontline professionals through the leaders and their organizations. CSSP targeted a handful of people with its first message; it targeted thousands of people with the second one. Although the leaders and the frontlines were members of the same organizations, their immediate desires relative to the new approach varied and, therefore, the strategic message was reviewed and modified as needed at each point of the rollout process.

Target Audiences May Be Channels, Not Actors

Not all target audiences are made up of people who can actually take the specific action that the organization wants taken. Remember that the purpose of messaging is to effect—or *cause to have happen*—the action the organization desires.

Sometimes, those who can cause something to happen may not be the same as those who do the acting. The St. Mary's Community Foundation might target high school guidance counselors because they urge deserving low-income students to apply for one of the foundation's scholarships. The Nashville chapter of the American Cancer Society might target adult children as an audience in a campaign to persuade older men to get prostate cancer exams because their children might be the most effective means of getting aging fathers to a doctor. The Lake Street Church might target local police because they can direct homeless people to eat at its soup kitchen.

An old, but still dramatic, example of this occurred in the 1980s when President Reagan's secretary of the Department of the Interior announced that he was going to open the nation's federally protected wilderness areas to oil and gas exploration. The Wilderness Society wanted Congress to act to forbid the secretary's initiative. Part of the Wilderness Society's strategy was to mobilize newspaper editorial writers throughout the country to editorialize against the plan as a way of pressuring their states' U.S. senators to stop it. The Wilderness Society knew that each newspaper would want to know how much oil and gas might be found in the wilderness areas in his or her own specific state. Just before the Senate was to address the issue, the Wilderness Society sent each state's major newspapers research data showing how much oil or gas could be found in the wilderness areas of their state. In every instance, the amount was negligible. As a result, 305 newspapers in 45 states ran editorials within a three-week period leading up to the Senate's consideration of the plan. Almost three-quarters of the editorials took the same position: don't allow it. Another 12 percent proposed a compromise. Even in Western states that usually were supportive of resource development, newspapers overwhelmingly opposed the idea. It was stopped dead. With the editorial writers, the Wilderness Society targeted a group that could not vote to stop the oil and gas drilling but could—and did—effect exactly that action.

For cause-related organizations, the news media is frequently a target audience. For social service organizations, local government agencies are frequent target audiences. Doctors and hospitals are often audiences for groups trying to reach specific sectors of the public with health-related education.

Limit the Number of Target Audiences

Some nonprofit organizations—often ones that are cause-related or provide social services—struggle with the task of choosing a few audiences to focus on. Most strategic message development processes include a discussion about how the issue being addressed is too important to limit the number of audiences to just a handful. The truth is that, unless groups do limit themselves, few will hear them.

As with other aspects of strategic message development, less is more when it comes to the total number of target audiences. It is fine to have one target audience. It is not fine to have five or ten target audiences. In most instances, an organization should limit itself to no more than three.

In truth, only two or three audiences will get much attention regardless of how many are selected and have subset messages created for them. As demonstrated by the table on page 39, it is simply too difficult to remember more than three messages. In 2003, a national foundation brought together three projects that had similar missions to see if a message could be created that would advance the common concept underlying them. Although the projects had common missions, they were structured in ways that required them to activate different groups to achieve their goals. As a result, they ended up with eight target audiences—too many to engage with successfully. In practice, they worked mainly with two or three of the audiences, but even then the diffusion of focus limited the effort's success somewhat.

In addition to the difficulty of remembering messages for five, seven, or ten target audiences, most organizations are limited in their ability to communicate with a large number of target audiences because their resources are too limited. When an organization lacks the resources to communicate its messages effectively to all the audiences it identifies, it is foolish to weaken its messages by creating language that attempts to speak to them all.

Although it is necessary to limit the number of audiences for a strategic message, groups may choose not to reduce their final audience choices until the end of the next step. As will be seen in the next chapter, audiences ultimately cluster by desire, so a single target audience may be created from a group of audiences identified in this step. For example, a disease-fighting organization might cluster volunteers, board of directors, and staff into an "internal" audience; create an "external" audience of members, donors, and policymakers; and group researchers, medical institutions, and medical funders into a "researchers" audience.

Usually the target audiences for a strategic message are fairly obvious, and brainstorming quickly surfaces the most important ones. Continued brainstorming can be useful, at times, because it uncovers a strategically important audience that was not obvious at first. However, in other instances, it does little but create a wish list of every person or group that might one day, in some way, take a minor action that advances the cause. In these situations, a team usually abruptly stops brainstorming when reminded that, for every named target audience, it will have to identify that group's constellation of desires in step three.

Summary

- Target audiences are made up of the people who must act if an organization is to achieve the goal of its strategic message.

- A target audience may be composed of those who are channels for reaching people who must act, not the actors themselves.

- There should be a limited number of target audiences, preferably no more than three.

- In the process of achieving a goal, audiences may change.

Discussion Questions

1. Are the target audiences we identified people who can cause the action we want?

2. To cause the action we want, can we go directly to the actors, or do we need to reach out to an intermediary audience that can prompt the actors to act?

3. Is one of our audiences "the public" or a similarly unattainable group—that is, have we defined our audiences too broadly?

4. Have we limited ourselves to three audiences? If not, is it because we think some of them will cluster into a single audience before we finish?

6. *Step Three*
Identify Audience Desires

SELF-INTEREST drives listening.

Politicians know it. Car salesmen know it. Casanovas know it. If you want me to listen, talk to me about something *I* care about. What *I* care about, not what you want me to care about.

And when you start talking to me, begin where I am. Meet me where I am and bring me toward you. Don't start talking *at* me from where you are. Learn from therapists, diplomats, and ministers—the good ones all operate from this perspective.

There is a shift in mental orientation during the message development process once the target audiences have been identified. Steps one and two of the process begin where *you* are—by identifying what action *your organization* wants and the audiences it needs to activate to achieve that action. However, once those decisions are made, the focus of message development changes from being about your organization to being about the target audiences. In step three, the organizational mind-set needs to shift from where it is to where its audiences are.

Message success depends on this reorientation of an organization's thinking. An example of this comes from the early childhood education field. In the mid-1980s, parents became fixated on their children's school success at increasingly early ages; they desired assurance that their young children wouldn't start out behind when they entered elementary school. A national association of early childhood professionals grew concerned when schools started testing kindergarteners to determine if they should be promoted to first grade. The association wanted parents to join them in fighting this trend among school systems, but they realized that overly concerned parents might support the unwise practice because they didn't know that such testing of very young children would probably return inaccurate information. When they sought parents' help to combat the trend, they used the parents' desire for school success as a point of persuasion. Their message was: *testing too early means failing too soon and flunking kindergarten could have damaging effects on a child's subsequent success in school.*

Another example comes from the same period but from a different early childhood organization. This group was concerned that parents were so obsessed with the intellectual development of their babies and toddlers that they missed the greater importance of the children's social and emotional development. They knew that young children who do not develop the social and emotional capabilities needed to handle the nonintellectual challenges of school—such as taking turns, following directions, getting along with others—do not fulfill their academic potential. The organization realized, however, that they needed to meet the parents where they were and try to bring them to the organization's understanding. Part of their message was converted to this slogan, which appeared on t-shirts and bags for several years: *to grow a child's mind, nurture a baby's heart.*

Many associations, foundations, and nonprofits fail to make this shift. After identifying their target audiences, they next ask themselves *what do we need to tell our audiences to get what we want?* Instead, they should be asking *what desires of our audiences are met if they act as we want them to?* As Sam Deep and Lyle Sussman put it, "Instead of focusing on what you're trying to get them to do, start focusing on what's in it for them if they do it."[18]

Chris DeCardy, now vice president and director of communications at the David and Lucile Packard Foundation, said it slightly differently when he was a media specialist working for environmental groups: "If you know the people you need to reach and know what they like, give it to them. The great thing about the environment is that it's all around us and means different things to different people. If we weren't so hung up on winning for 'our' reasons, we'd be smarter about listening to everyone else's reasons and appealing to them."[19]

Identifying what motivates a target audience is as much an art as a science. Remember—organizations tend to focus on what an audience needs, but an audience is more likely to be motivated by what it wants. Organizations may believe that they cannot determine an audience's self-interest because they lack the resources to do commercial-style market research, yet simply listening well at every opportunity returns valuable understanding.

Strategic messaging requires focusing on the self-interest of target audiences, but it does not mean abandoning the organization's own self-interest. Remember the Action Connection diagram: the centerpiece of strategic message development is found in the overlap between what the organization desires and what target audiences desire.

Audiences Cluster by Common Desire

Target audiences or target markets can be defined in many ways. Many nonprofits classify people by demographic factors such as age, income, geography, race, or religion. Others differentiate audiences based on lifestyle characteristics such as whether people frequently attend cultural or sporting events. Still others use factors such as a propensity to adopt new practices quickly or slowly. However, when defining audiences for purposes of strategic messaging, nonprofits, foundations, and associations should cluster people based on their desires rather than on other factors.

When defining audiences for purposes of strategic messaging, cluster people based on their desires rather than on demographic or lifestyle factors.

As noted previously, desire motivates action, and action is the goal of a strategic message. To motivate action successfully, a strategic message must communicate the satisfaction of audience desire; segmentation based on differing desire, therefore, is critical.

This differentiation by desire is key because people take the same action for very different reasons. One person washes his car to maintain its finish because he wants to get top dollar when he trades it in. Another washes hers because she likes to project a sporty image. A third washes the car because that's the price his father exacts if he wants to use it to take his friends out on Saturday night. Same action, different desires.

The same dynamic holds true with charitable activities. One volunteer shows up for the church's Habitat for Humanity project because he wants to help a family less fortunate than his. Another, who also likes to help people, shows up for the same project because she wants to learn how to make home repairs through hands-on experience. Still another volunteers because he is lonely and wants to meet people who enjoy, as he does, lending a hand to others. Same action, different desires.

Sharply focusing on the desire of a potential audience can lead to surprises at times. Two examples from actual client experience illustrate how seemingly identical groups of people are, when viewed through the lens of motivating desire, actually quite different.

- In a large mid-Atlantic city, an organization sought funding to continue a program supportive of local social entrepreneurs. Its two target audiences for obtaining donations were wealthy individuals and family foundations. The organization realized that the two groups were not motivated by the same primary desires even when the money came from the same familial source. As successful entrepreneurs, the wealthy individuals wanted to help risk-takers and innovators like themselves when they donated directly. However, through their foundations, they wanted to see that their philanthropic investments were returning value; thus, their foundations funded programs that had proven their worth. The different desires of these audiences meant that the subset messages to the wealthy individuals differed from those aimed at foundation staff.

- A few years ago, the State Government Management Initiative (SGMI)[20] created a message to persuade influential individuals in government to use information that it had developed to change state practices and policies.

It first divided state government leaders by those who were elected and those who were not. Upon reflection, however, SGMI realized that the real differentiating factor was not how a leader had been put into his or her position but whether the individual was motivated primarily by political factors such as re-election or by management factors such as having access to best practices on a range of management issues. It recognized that some appointed executives were motivated primarily by a desire to improve agency effectiveness rather than by political concerns, even though their jobs depended on the governor's re-election. Conversely, some career employees sought to advance through political connections and were motivated more by political factors than management ones. SGMI would almost never know if a specific individual fit into one category or the other, but it did know that it had to communicate in such a way that each audience heard a compelling message.

Differentiating audiences based on common desire rather than a certain demographic or lifestyle aspect has a parallel in the corporate world. An article in the *Harvard Business Review* in 2005 urged companies to segment markets based on what job was being done by the product that purchasers bought, not by traditional factors such as age, gender, and so forth.[21] The example they used was a fast food company that wanted to determine who was buying its milk shakes so that it could develop a strategy for selling more shakes. It wondered whether buyers were categorizable by age, gender, occupation, parental status, or any of a number of other classifications. Through observational research followed by individual interviews, the company discovered that milk shake purchasers were not differentiated in any of those ways. To its great surprise, it discovered that most milk shakes were purchased in the morning—by workers who had long, boring commutes and desired a product that would get them through their commute without getting the steering wheel sticky, and a product filling enough to get them through their 10 a.m. hunger attack. Buyers had usually experimented with other breakfast products, like bagels, and found those did not do the job. Said another way, the products did not fulfill their desire.

Audience Differentiation by Desire:
Different Desires, Sitting Side by Side

In the late 1990s, the Nebraska Health and Human Services System (NHHSS) undertook the most far-reaching reorganization ever attempted by the state government. It sought to reconfigure the delivery of health and human services statewide to achieve better integration of services and greater prevention of the need for services. The change required realigning the work of 5,000 health and human services professionals who served 400,000 people.

The restructuring meant that frontline workers would have to change virtually all aspects of their work life: their work identity, the structure of their work life, their relationships with clients and peers, the rewards and sanctions for success and failure, and their work culture. For example, staff would now function as generalists, not specialists. Before the reconfiguration, staff had dealt with only a client's specific issue, such as welfare or juvenile justice. Staff would now handle all of a client's needs. Staff's orientation to their clients would need to change from simply helping them, to motivating them to help themselves. Staff would have more long-term relationships with clients rather than short-term ones. They would be evaluated less on how many people they served and more on the outcome of their service.

After NHHSS made the necessary changes at state headquarters to support the reorganization, it turned its attention to telling frontline staff that the time had come for their work to change. When a message development team began discussing the audiences, it realized that frontline workers were not a homogenous target audience, but two audiences. They did not split by factors such as where in the state they worked, what sort of job they held, or how long they had been working for the system. The frontline workers were grouped by those who saw this change as an opportunity—the O group—and those who saw it as a threat—the T group. Messages needed to be developed that allowed the O group to hear that their desire to change the system in positive ways was being met. At the same time, messages were needed that allowed the T group to hear that their perception—change is hard and we need support in making those changes—was not being ignored. The team created an overarching core message that was the same, of course, for both groups: *NHHSS has created a sufficient foundation that we can now accelerate our transformation to an integrated service delivery system.*

(continued)

However, the workers' differing orientation to change required that different subset messages be created for each group. Following are two examples of those subset messages:

One subset message addressed the change in work orientation. For the O group the message was: *It's time to do what you've always said needed to be done: serve people, not deliver programs.* The same subset message for the T group was: *You're being required to make basic changes in ways that you have been working for a long time, and we realize that is hard.*

One subset message addressed the change in relationships with clients. For the O audience the message was: *Finally, you're expected to engage fully with the client—understand all the needs so you can serve all the needs.* For the T audience the message was: We *recognize you're being asked to broaden your involvement with clients and often to engage with them in new ways. We will provide training to help you do that.*

Of course NHHSS couldn't know where each of its 5,000 workers stood on the issue of change—whether they fell in the O group or T group. And people who were exposed to these differing messages were often sitting next to each other in an office. Therefore, there was no way to segregate the message delivery so that the O group got only the O subset messages and the T group only the T messages. Remember, however, that *self-interest drives listening.* In other words, this problem was not really a problem because people tend to hear messages that resonate most closely with their desires and ignore those that don't, so long as the messages are not substantially in conflict. Both groups connect with the core message because it speaks to their mutual interest. The subset messages speak to each group's specific interest, but they could be delivered simultaneously because the T and O groups self-segregated, each paying attention to the subset message that most addressed their orientation.

Desire Trumps Need

Nonprofit organizations focus on what they believe others need like dogs focus on bones—with consuming attention. Associations believe members need to read the e-mail newsletter to keep current with the latest professional developments. Environmentalists believe homeowners need to lower their thermostats in the winter to conserve energy and reduce the demand for oil. Government agencies believe that high school students need to "just say no" to sex, and drinking, and drugs, and driving while talking on their cell phones, and . . . .

With most people, however, want is frequently a stronger motivator to action than need. We all *need* to exercise, but the desire not to spend time exercising exceeds the need to be fit, which is why Goodwill stores often boast a selection of near-new rowing machines and exercise bikes. People do not need to build houses on fragile coastlines, but they do anyway because they want the beach at their doorstep.

We are reminded of the power of desire with every advertisement we see. Sex sells beer. Prestige sells cars. Beauty sells soap.

Need is often easier to determine than audience desire. A needs assessment can tell an organization the number of illiterate adults who live in the city, however, it may be harder to determine what desire might motivate these adults to attend literacy classes.

Even in situations where there appears to be a need that "obviously" determines the thrust of the strategic message, message developers need to be sensitive to powerful desires and speak to them. Anti-smoking activists ultimately realized that telling teenagers that smoking can kill you had limited value because young people feel invincible; however, talking about the fact that smoking makes one's breath stink and therefore others don't want to kiss you *was* a message that hit on a motivating desire. In the same vein, even though diabetics need annual hemoglobin tests to protect against complications like foot amputation, it might be more effective to speak to the desires that would go unrealized if a foot were amputated: a grandfather might feel less able chase after his grandchildren, an expert horsewoman might no longer compete in horse shows.

One reason nonprofits, foundations, and associations focus on audience needs is that they are often easier to determine than audience desires. A needs assessment can tell an organization the approximate number of illiterate adults who live in the city and whether classes should focus on native English speakers or non-native speakers. It may be harder, however, to determine what desire might motivate these adults to *attend* literacy classes.

Determining Desire:
The Market Research Challenge

It is a challenge for nonprofits, foundations, and associations to find out what people desire. Sometimes people don't know what they want. What is the most common response when you ask your kids what they want for dinner or your spouse what she wants to do on Friday night? *I don't know.*

Other times, people won't reveal their true motivations for a variety of reasons—distrust, desire for privacy, fear of appearing selfish, fear of embarrassment, peer pressure, and so forth. Few politicians will admit that they voted for a bill because they wanted to get re-elected. A retirement-age founder/CEO might say he's still needed at the organization, but really continues working to retain his status as an important figure in his community. A mother who volunteers her time at the local library may not admit she's there to take a break from her four rambunctious children.

However, just because it is difficult to learn what people want does not mean that it can be neglected.

There are innumerable ways to gather information. Conferences provide ready access to members who can be captured for informal focus groups or individual interviews in the halls. Monitoring member listservs provides another way to learn what members want. For social service agencies, asking clients to answer a few questions on a postage-paid postcard can supply useful information. Monitoring leading blogs on a particular issue area may help keep an organization abreast of attitudes in the sector. Periodic debriefing of staff—especially receptionists and others on the front lines of member, client, and customer contact—can reveal important information or impressions. Creativity may be more significant than money when identifying how to capture information about target audiences.

Observational market research is having a resurgence in corporate America, and it can be equally valuable in the nonprofit sector. Companies are returning to the technique because they have discovered that customers sometimes cannot articulate why they want something, so surveys can be of limited value in certain circumstances. Agencies and associations might discover that the technique has utility for them, too. If Kimberly-Clark Corporation can hire researchers to watch parents interact with their toddlers so the company can improve Huggies diapers, perhaps a family support center might improve their services if they planted a trained volunteer in the reception area to observe the interactions of different clients, listen to them talk to each other, and have follow-up conversations. If Moen Inc. can observe people in the shower (they used nudist volunteers) as a way to better understand what people want in a showerhead, perhaps an association might learn more about what conference vendors want by closely watching and listening as they set up in the exhibit hall. The technique is limited only by the creativity of the organization, and by its commitment to learning as much as possible about what motivates its constituents.

Strategic messages frequently target internal audiences as well as external ones, so it is important to gather information on internal audiences too. Properly conducted exit interviews, using open-ended questions, may deliver information not just on unmet desires of departing staff but also, secondhand, on the desires of existing staff. CEOs can discover useful information by including brainstorming sessions in senior management meetings because brainstorming is good for getting information in an unthreatening way. Organization leaders can ask managers what they want to talk about and then listen, rather than responding immediately. Another simple means to gather information is for a supervisor to ask, at annual performance evaluations, if there is anything he could do to make the staff member's job easier. Expect the unexpected—and not necessarily the difficult. One manager who routinely asked her staff this question was told by a worker that he'd like her to write her notes to him on full-size paper so he wouldn't lose them so easily on his desk—a simple desire that would never have been known without asking.

Determining Desire:
The Organizational Culture Challenge

The operating culture of a nonprofit is often a bigger impediment to discovering audience desire than lack of time, money, or market-research expertise. A dearth of interest in learning what their audiences want is more crippling than a dearth of resources. Although organizations cannot control an audience's unwillingness to reveal their true motivations or their inability to articulate desires, nonprofits can control the other side of the problem: the organization's lack of curiosity.

Organizations must change from having *telling* cultures to having *asking* cultures if they want to be effective in today's world of increasing personal power. Asking questions is the only way to keep their finger on the pulse of their audiences, which is essential for developing strategic messages (not to mention designing outreach strategies, creating effective programs, and conducting other key activities).

The receptionist asks *Is there other information you'd like?* after getting a new caller's request. The media relations specialist provides a reporter with requested information and slips in a quick question before saying good-bye: *What do you want that you aren't getting from us?* The executive director encounters a volunteer in the grocery store and asks *Are we supporting you as a volunteer in the ways you want us to?* The board president bumps into a major donor at the symphony and asks *Are you getting all that you want from us?*

In organizations with an asking culture, each staff member and volunteer believes that the organization's success depends on connecting solidly with important constituencies. And, the best way to connect with constituents is to know what they want. In an asking culture, every conversation with a stakeholder contains the potential for gathering important market data. Every stakeholder is seen as a contributor to the organization's knowledge, not a drain on its time. In that culture, every staff member is a market researcher and each embraces the importance of asking what a constituent wants. In an asking culture, people know that effective communication and successful operations depend as much on how well you listen as on how well you speak.

Knowing the Need, Discovering the Desire

Too much knowledge can be a dangerous thing. Certainly that can be true when organizations with expert knowledge struggle to share their knowledge with the people they wish to influence. The organizations care so much about their audiences hearing what they need to know, that they cannot bring themselves to deliver information that their audiences desire to know and will most likely influence their behavior.

An example of this occurred when ZERO TO THREE, an internationally recognized expert in the social and emotional development of young children, began in the mid-1990s to reach out to parents. For its first twenty years, ZERO TO THREE had focused on providing professionals with the latest research findings on the development of babies and toddlers.

The organization decided it needed help developing a message for its new audience. The problem, as staff saw it, was not that they didn't know what to say to parents, but that they couldn't agree on what was most important to say. At a meeting of the board—twenty-five eminent scholars, research scientists, and practitioners in the field—each board member was asked to write down the single most important thing that parents needed to know to raise children who were emotionally and socially healthy.

As would happen in virtually any organization with similarly expert board members, there was little unanimity about the single most important item. That painful discovery prompted the organization to fall back on asking parents what they most wanted to know.

To uncover that information, ZERO TO THREE put the board through another process and identified eight to ten of the most important messages parents needed to hear. It then garnered specific funding and used those messages as the basis for discussion in eight focus groups in four cities. Brought into focus by those eight discussions, survey questions were designed and a thousand-person public survey was conducted to determine what parents most wanted to know.

The result: parents most wanted to know how to be sure their child was normal. Their biggest fear was that they would miss seeing something important about their baby in time to correct it. Not one of the experts had identified that specific desire as being the most important issue to address.

(continued)

Parents also said, however, that they had no time to read another baby book or watch another baby video.

To its credit, ZERO TO THREE listened to what parents said they wanted and designed and delivered their message in a way that parents could absorb. They developed materials that helped parents understand what to expect from their babies and toddlers and how to support their normal development, and they delivered it on the back of cereal boxes and in other creative ways. For example, they produced a colorful growth chart for hanging on the wall, so parents could measure their child's increasing height (without scarring the doorjamb with pencil marks). Floating around the measuring stick were short blurbs on what normal behavior looked like, in three-month increments, from birth through age three. In the minute it took to mark their toddler's growth, parents could absorb what normal development at that age looked like. ZERO TO THREE took the critical information that experts felt parents needed and delivered it within the context of what parents said they wanted. Both the organization and parents achieved their desires.

Granted, this kind of organizational change takes practice. Organizations, like their audiences, are driven by self-interest. They continually monitor and respond to what they need to do and how they are going to marshal money and energy to get everything done. We train ourselves to focus tightly so that we are efficient and effective, knowing that without clear and consistent focus on our priorities, we stand little chance of succeeding in a highly competitive world. Under these conditions, it is almost an unnatural act to stop, refocus, and talk to our target audiences from their perspective, not ours.

The ultimate responsibility for creating an asking culture rests with the executive director and senior staff. Leadership is critical to building an environment of questioning. Organizational leaders model the orientation and, through insistence, encourage the change. For example, new program ideas are met with the question *Is this what our constituents want—and how do we know that?* Leadership creates mechanisms that encourage staff to ask questions as a routine part of business. Leadership also institutes systems that channel responses into decision-making processes. Remember, if you had a reason for getting the information, you have a reason for using it.

While leadership is key to transforming an organization into an asking culture, savvy communicators—found in communications, marketing, fundraising, membership, public policy, and similar departments—can play a critical role in pushing for such culture change if management gives them that power. Skilled communicators are customer-centric rather than organization-centric. They are as focused on achieving organizational goals as anyone else, but they more frequently recognize that the best way to do that may be to look at the world from the perspective of the target audience, aka the customer. When developing a message, they operate less from a sales orientation—here's what I want you to buy—than from a marketing orientation, which asks *what do you want?* The following table shows the difference between the two approaches:

Sales Versus Marketing Orientations

Sales Orientation	Marketing Orientation
Focus is primarily on what the organization wants to tell its audiences.	Focus is primarily on how the organization can speak so that it connects with its audiences' desires.
Primary task is to persuade the audience to "buy" the organization's offering, that is, support its idea, use its service, or purchase its product.	Primary task is to find out what the audience wants relative to what the organization is offering.
Assumption is that the organization is right in its approach and the key need is to inform its audiences.	Assumption is that the organization is right but will be ignored unless its offering connects with audience desire.
The challenge is getting the audience to understand the issue sufficiently to recognize why it needs what the organization is offering.	The challenge is getting the audience to hear that one of its desires will be met by "buying" what the organization is offering.
Message must be clear, concise, and convincing.	Message must be clear, concise, and connect to the audience's desire in a compelling manner.

When the difficulty of determining desire is added to organizations' inclination to tell people what they need, it is small wonder that many organizations have trouble focusing on audience desire. Yet not focusing on desire promises that the messages will fail to achieve the organization's goal. Choosing to focus on audience need rather than desire, because need is easier to determine, is like buying milk at the grocery rather than charcoal because milk is easier to find; when you get home, you're no closer to being able to grill your hamburgers than when you left.

Summary

- People listen to messages that speak to their self-interest.

- People are motivated more by desire than by need.

- Target audiences cluster based on common desires.

- Organizations learn what their audiences desire by asking—in a variety of ways.

Discussion Questions

1. Do we group our target audiences by their desires or in some other way, such as demographic factors?

2. In choosing target audiences, have we focused on their common needs or on their common desires?

3. How have we ascertained the desires of our audiences? Can we establish processes that allow us to capture better information about our audiences' desires in the future?

4. Are we so focused on telling our audiences what they need that we fail, routinely and consistently, to ask them what they want?

5. If we are asking our audiences what they want, are we integrating that information into our decision-making processes so that our decisions are actually informed by that information?

6. When we design our communications, do we begin with the perspective that we are right and that our biggest challenge is simply to get our audiences to recognize this and take the action we urge?

7. *Step Four*
Find the Mutuality

THE KEY TO A SUCCESSFUL strategic message is mutual satisfaction of desire.

After an organization has determined what action it desires, what people it needs to activate to satisfy that desire, and what those people want, it moves to step four and confronts the moment of truth in strategic message development: is there a connection between what the organization wants and what its target audiences want? Can the audience meet our desire and can we meet theirs? Where is mutual satisfaction to be found?

Note, that we seek mutual *satisfaction,* not mutual desire. An organization and its target audiences may support the same action, but their reasons for doing so may differ. An association wants its members to take a course to keep current with professional practices; some members take the course to become more proficient, others—perhaps many others—take it because having the course completion certificate on their office wall will impress clients. The city orchestra wants to launch a program to expose inner-city children to classical music; a wealthy music lover sponsors the program because he is looking for a highly visible community project with which to associate himself. A community development group wants the city council to loosen restrictive zoning regulations; in a campaign year, the city council chair ushers the change through the process because she hopes it will spur business development *and* because satisfying people helps her re-election prospects. A consumer group wants the *Los Angeles Times* to do an expose on falsely labeled organic vegetables; a reporter for the paper writes a story because she is looking for a front-page byline.

Many nonprofit organizations, especially those that are cause-related, fail to create effective messages because they want their target audiences to take action for the right reasons. The right reasons, of course, being the reasons that the organization believes are right. Some people call this self-righteous. Some call it naive. Here, it's just called the fastest route to communication failure.

Messages That Generate Action

Can an audience meet our desire and can we meet theirs? The place where that becomes obvious is the fourth step of strategic message development: the Action Connection. The organization knows what action it wants and what resources it has available to try to achieve that action. It mentally draws a circle around that knowledge. It has identified who its target audiences are and what their desires are. It mentally draws a circle around that knowledge. Do the circles overlap? Is there a place where the action the organization is willing to elicit overlaps with what its target audiences want?

The diagram is the moment of truth. Either there is a connection between the organization's desire and its audiences' desires, or there is not. If there is an overlap, a successful strategic message can be created. If there is not, it can't.

The Action Connection

PLACE WHERE A STRATEGIC MESSAGE IS CREATED

ORGANIZATION DESIRE   SHARED DESIRE   AUDIENCE DESIRE

Following are some examples of how organization and audience desires can overlap:

- The local hospice is trying to increase its visibility in the community. It hears that the Visiting Nurses Association is looking for materials to help some of its clients deal with end-of-life issues. Their desires overlap, and the hospice decides to focus on the association as one of its target audiences for its outreach campaign.

- The League of Women Voters wants volunteers to do voter registration in retirement homes, and one of the League members knows that the Actively Retired Club is looking to expand its membership. The League sees an overlap of desire. It enlists Actively Retired Club members to staff voter registration tables in the retirement homes' dining rooms each evening for a week, and the club hands out promotional brochures for itself at the same time.

- The zoo and the local chapter of Freedom for Animals disagree on many issues. However, they share a desire to discourage parents from giving exotic baby animals to children as gifts. For that reason, Freedom for Animals agrees to publicize the zoo's holiday message about not giving such gifts to children at Christmas.

Of course, there will always be organizational desires that do not fit in the overlap area, just as there will always be audience desires that are found outside the overlap. Lack of overlap is not a commentary on the validity of those desires. It simply means that those desires will not be formative in the message development process.

Mutuality May Require Strategic Decisions

Many times an organization confronts a strategic decision when the Action Connection is revealed. This is one reason why strategic messaging should involve top level executives in the organization. Sometimes, achieving an *overlap of desires* between the organization and its audiences requires a reallocation of resources by the organization. Here are some examples of decisions that organizations encounter:

- A professional association wants to develop a strategic message to encourage elementary school teachers to adopt new practices for teaching reading. A member survey shows the teachers are amenable to the changes if they have training to understand how to implement the changes. Money to develop training modules is not in the organization's current budget. The organization must decide whether its desire for the action is strong enough to prompt it to shift funds from another program to create the training materials.

- A human rights organization wants a committee of the United States Senate to hold hearings to investigate human rights abuses in a certain country, and it is developing a strategic message to editorial writers around the country urging them to write an editorial calling for senators to act. The organization's communications staff, however, is currently tied up developing a press campaign on another hot issue. The organization must decide if it should reassign staff to handle this issue first.

- A community organization is losing the major underwriter of a scholarship program that identifies and supports emerging visual artists. Other funders can be found to fill the void, but these funders want to participate in choosing the artists who are awarded grants. Is the organization willing to restructure its process to permit funders to be involved in the selection?

Mutuality May Reveal Organizational Surprises

The Action Connection is also a place where surprises sometimes occur. As mentioned earlier, once the strategic message development team has identified its audiences' desires, it is ready to decide which desires the organization can meet. To do so, team members must have a full understanding of the organization's priorities and what projects staff currently work on. Oftentimes, the suggestions are based on what team members believe staff are working on, based on the strategic plan, a board directive, or some other source. However, the organization may not, in fact, have executed the plan or board directive. In other words, it's not happening.

While not common, this is also not a rare occurrence in strategic message development. A board member finds out that what the board thought was a top priority of the organization is actually receiving scant attention. The head of one department learns that the work her staff is doing to achieve an objective in the strategic plan is not being supported by other departments. Department staff discover that an initiative they never even heard about is a major focus of another department. At this point, leaders of the board and staff often recognize that long-discussed changes in practices, priorities, or personnel must be acted on. For example:

- Fundraisers for a research program focused on analyzing economic factors that affect homebuying by six different Asian populations in the United States developed a list of potential donors for the program. The fundraisers began working with program staff to create a strategic message aimed at foundations and donors. To their dismay, the fundraisers learned that the researchers could not obtain reliable data on two of the Asian population groups, and as a result they had revised their research to focus on only four. Unfortunately, a major donor was interested in one of the populations the researchers had to drop. Losing that donor would have a disproportionately negative impact on the likelihood of being able to raise sufficient funds to undertake the project at all. Surprise.

- The personnel committee of the board of directors developed a new job-performance evaluation system. It decided to gather a senior executive team to develop a message that would persuade staff to accept the new system. It heard that staff wanted a more rational assignment of salary increases, and it believed the new system would meet that desire. In the course of discussing the overlap between what the board wanted and what the staff wanted, the committee discovered that job descriptions, which were a critical component in the system, were so outdated as to be almost useless. Launching the new system had to wait a year until job descriptions were made current. Surprise.

Reaffirm the Action

When the strategic message development team reaches the point where it understands the overlap of interests between the organization and its target audiences, it needs to pause to reconsider the action it originally set out to achieve. Is the action important enough to reallocate resources to deliver the message? Does it want to execute planned program changes so that it can meet its audiences' desires, or can it see now that the planned changes were ill-advised and will not help it achieve the organization's mission efficiently?

It is highly unlikely that an organization will totally abandon its message development at this point. Usually, strategic messages are developed because the desired action is very important to the organization. However, very occasionally, a strategic message development team will drop an audience or part of an audience from its targeted groups because the organization is unable or unwilling to make the changes required to meet that audience's desires. In doing so, it must recognize that dropping an audience or part of an audience may impede its ability to achieve the action it wants.

Summary

- The Action Connection diagram captures the essential truth of successful strategic messaging: an effective message is based on the mutual satisfaction of desire.

- Seek mutual *satisfaction*, not mutual desire. An organization and its target audiences may support the same action, but their reasons for doing so may differ.

- Finding the mutuality that is essential to successful strategic message development may require making programmatic changes.

- The search for mutuality may also reveal organizational surprises that call into question organizational operations or the initial goal of the strategic message.

Discussion Questions

1. Are we focusing on what we want as well as on what our audiences want?

2. To deliver what our audiences want and thus achieve our desired action, do we need to make changes in any programs, processes, or resource allocations?

3. Having determined what will be required to obtain the audience action we want, do we believe the action is important enough to merit the allocation of time, staff, funding, and other resources?

Step Five
Express the Message

NEVER WHISPER to the deaf or wink at the blind.

This Slovenian proverb captures the key to expressing a strategic message: put your message out in such a way that your target audience can take it in. Use words that they easily understand. Be brief so that they don't get lost. Limit the number of points you make so that they aren't overwhelmed. Speak to their desire.

Remember what the strategic message is designed to do. First, it captures the target audience's attention in that first minute you have to hook your listener, the minute when your audience gives you his or her attention or mentally (or perhaps even physically) drifts away. The audience catch must be done quickly, and therefore your words and thoughts must be few and carefully chosen. Second, the message structures the ensuing conversation, keeping you mindful of the audience's most important concerns, which are the ones that should be most expansively addressed. The discipline of a strategic message helps you remember, when addressing additional issues, to strive to talk about the issues in terms of the listener's interest.

Like other aspects of strategic message development, the necessity of expressing the message in a way that resonates with the target audiences—satisfies their desire and uses their language—may be fairly self-evident. However, some groups stumble in step five as they actually write the strategic message. They revert to a self-orientation, losing their sharp focus on their audiences. The result is that, in the final step of the process, they lose direction and fail to achieve their goal—like the marathoner who lost the Olympic gold medal by turning the wrong direction as he entered the stadium for the final lap.

Write from Their Point of View, Not Yours

When the time comes to express the strategic message in words, organizations often slip back into the mind-set of *What do we need to tell them?* They tend to "pontificate, not communicate," says Thea Lurie, former communications director at the Ford Foundation.[22] That approach is, of course, looking through the wrong end of the telescope. *What do they need to hear?* is the correct perspective.

In 2002, the National Association for the Education of Young Children (NAEYC) made this mistake in the first draft of its strategic message, but it caught and corrected the mistake before it finished. NAEYC was creating a message to support a new initiative: persuading child care professionals to build better relationships with families to prevent child abuse and neglect in the home and elsewhere. A NAEYC survey of early childhood professionals revealed that, by an overwhelming number, they were willing to take such steps if they had some additional training. These professionals did not want the additional responsibility without being prepared for it. Heartened by the survey results, NAEYC decided it would provide training assistance, and it began to craft a strategic message to the field urging acceptance of the new practices.

The first draft of its core message was a call to action: NAEYC called on professionals in the field to be more proactive in developing relationships with families as a means of preventing child abuse. Upon reflection, NAEYC recognized the error of this message. It had written a message that expressed only what it wanted, forgetting that the survey had revealed that professionals were willing to adopt new practices if they received training to help them know what to do. NAEYC rewrote the core message to speak to that critical audience desire. It read: *Early childhood educators are willing to be even more active in preventing child abuse and neglect. NAEYC is leading an effort to help them.*

Remember, what people need to hear in a strategic message is that some desire of theirs is met by taking the action you wish. They need to hear this in language that they understand and might use themselves. What people need to hear is information they comprehend easily.

Life is littered with examples of organizations that fail to achieve their goals because they communicated information from their point of view, not from their audience's perspective. Just to cite one: in the early 1990s, the water department of a Western city used a billboard campaign that called on households to limit their water use to one hundred gallons a day. But there was one problem: no one knew how much they used already. Most people thought they only used about ten gallons a day. The campaign failed because people ignored the message, thinking it didn't apply to them.

Speaking the Audience's Language

In the early days of community foundations, when they were not well understood by the general public, the Arlington (Virginia) Community Foundation sought to create a strategic message to strengthen its institutional identity. It did not use the term "community foundation" in its core or subset messages, even though the term would have made the message shorter, because the term meant nothing to Arlington donors. The foundation knew that building an understanding of the term would take time. In the interim, however, the organization needed a quick way to open conversational doors with its target audiences. It needed a strategic message. This was the core message the foundation created: *We are building a permanent reservoir of charitable funds to ensure that Arlington remains the community we treasure.*

In eighteen words, the organization captured its essence—*a permanent reservoir of charitable funds*—as well as the desire of its target donors, which was *to ensure that Arlington remains the community we treasure.* In describing itself, the foundation used words that were not only accurate, but spoke to the desires of its target audiences for an "insurance policy" for Arlington's future. Permanent spoke to the desire of many donors to leave a legacy to the community they loved. Reservoir suggested that the money would be there to support worthy causes even when times were tough and other funders had run dry.

Use Their Words, Not Yours

You've seen the highway sign: *Speed kills.* There should be a messaging sign: Jargon kills. Words that your organization uses every day are often not quickly understood by your target audiences. In today's oversaturated communications environment, if messages are not quickly understood they are ignored. Using jargon kills your chances of being heard.

Jargon may be technical terms used in your discipline. For example, foundations and nonprofit consultants use the term "capacity building" to refer to an array of services that improve an organization's ability to go about its business. The term has meaning for them, but often not for others. Public health organizations use the terms "substance abuse" and "chemical dependency" to indicate behaviors that include the addictive use of drugs, including alcohol—terms that many people would not understand.

Jargon may be common words that have a different meaning in the context of your profession. For example, in this book, the term "strategic message" is very specific; it is jargon that may have meant little to you when you started reading this book. An oft-used bit of jargon among many nonprofits and association is the use of the term "community" to broadly include groups of people of like interest or type—such as the "nonprofit community." To many people, the word "community" more readily conveys the meaning of neighborhood. (Note that since "nonprofit" is also a form of jargon, "nonprofit community" is bewildering for those unfamiliar with the language.)

Jargon may be phrases that have become shorthand, within your professional or political community, for a whole body of knowledge or for a philosophical position. For example, many people, even among those working for environmental or religious organizations, may not know that the term "ecotheology" denotes a variety of perspectives existing at the junction of faith and ecology.

Jargon may also be acronyms or shorthand that have little meaning outside their place of use. For example, "LGBT" is meaningful to people involved with the politics of civil rights for people who identify themselves as lesbian, gay, bisexual, or transgender, but this term may not be known to others. "FAQ" is known to many people as shorthand for "frequently asked questions," but would be meaningless to people who do not use the Internet often. Your organization may commonly refer to itself by its initials, or by one word from its entire name, but audiences won't know that when you say "I-F-E-J" or "I-fedge," or "the Institute," that you are referring to the Institute for Ending Jargon.

Inevitably, someone in a strategic message development group will argue for the necessity of including a specific jargon term in the message. *There is no other way of saying it* is often one lament. *They'll understand what it means when they finish the sentence* is another. *If we don't use the phrase, the message will be too long* is a third. None of these is an acceptable reason for creating a strategic message that an audience will ignore. Message development teams have to wrestle hard against these temptations and simply keep working until they succeed in crafting messages that will be heard.

Regrettably, one reason that some groups drag their feet in jettisoning specialized language is because they fear that they will look less competent to colleagues in the field. The following is the only exception to the no-jargon rule: using jargon may be legitimate if colleagues in the field are the only target audience and if not using it would interfere with the strategic message's impact. If these conditions do not exist, then message developers must resist falling victim to a big messaging hazard—institutional ego—and shun the jargon.

Plain English, Please

Many nonprofits have been using jargon so long that they think everyone understands and uses these phrases. With thanks to Tony Proscio and the Edna McConnell Clark Foundation for their crusade for clarity, ask yourself which of these terms your neighbor would use:

Technical assistance or *expert advice?*

Capacity building or *more money, more computers, more expertise?*

Devise metrics or *measure?*

Be proactive or *take the initiative?*

Learnings or *information, knowledge, understanding?*

Different modalities or *different methods, different ways?*

A great web site is "The Jargon Files" at http://www.emcf.org/pub/jargon/

Less Is More

At the beginning of a strategic message development process, most associations and nonprofits do not believe they can capture what they need to say in a core message of twenty to thirty words or in just three subset points per audience. They insist that the issues they deal with are too complex, their array of services and products are too diverse, or their vision is too complicated. Few groups disagree with the goal of expressing the message concisely, but they almost uniformly assert that it is not possible for them.

As mentioned earlier, brevity is critically important. A strategic message is designed to catch the audience's attention; a listener may give you fifteen to twenty seconds and a reader may give you less. If your core message hooks your audience, you have the rest of the minute to deliver your subset message. If you still have the audience's attention after that first fateful minute, then you can shift from the catch to a conversation.

Not only should the words be few, the points that are made in the strategic message need to be strictly limited as well. As shown in Chapter 3, the mind cannot deal with more than three variables at a time and still retain the information that you are trying to transmit. Your mind will have trouble remembering more than the three most important points you want to deliver. Assuredly, your audience's mind will not absorb more than three points before some of them begin to be lost. The question then becomes, Would you rather decide which points your listener "loses" by excluding those extra points before you open your mouth, or do you trust your listener to forget only those points that you consider least important?

Keeping a core message short is a particular challenge when an organization needs to communicate ideas that appear to be in conflict, which is not uncommon. An association wants to play up the size of its membership (to get across the idea that *this is the organization to join*), the depth of its product line (to assert that *you'll find whatever you need here*), and the speed of its order fulfillment (to promise *we'll get you what you need, fast*). However, it also wants to convey its commitment to treating each member as an individual and providing the personal attention that one expects from a boutique-size association. How does it do that in twenty-five words?

Conflicting Needs, Same Message

Several years ago a renowned West Coast medical center had a business problem: it needed to market itself to patients without undercutting its marketing to funders. The center's groundbreaking medical discoveries drew patients from throughout the United States and around the world and resulted in a steady flow of grant money for further research. However, its research required a hospital in which to treat patients, and grant money did not cover hospital services. To cover those costs, it needed paying patients. It faced the same marketing challenge that any community hospital does: how to fill enough hospital beds each day to keep the center solvent.

How could it promote itself as pioneering, which was essential to its research funding, as well as caring, which was essential to attracting patients? Moreover, how could it derive marketing value with patients when much of the center's research was basic, not applied, and therefore at least one step removed from patient treatment? Health professionals know that basic research provids the knowledge that is transformed into therapies to help patients, but few nonmedical people make that connection. So how could the medical center help potential patients realize that the center's pioneering basic research helped them achieve their desire of better health?

The complexity of the challenge seemed to promise that a core message would not be written. Yet it was—although it ran longer than optimal. This was what the center adopted as a core message: *Our scientists and clinicians are determined to improve people's lives—and they do. We pioneer a field and remain on its leading edge until the discoveries of our labs make a difference in the lives of our patients.*

The beginning and end of the message focuses on patients, while the center positions the medical center as a pioneer and conveys its commitment to research that makes a difference in peoples' lives.

Not easily. It takes hours of hard discussion to peel away the layers of what is being discussed so that the group can home in ever more precisely on the heart of the matter—the irreducible core. It usually causes noticeable frustration, irritation, and sometimes anger as colleagues wrangle over what really is the essential matter. In almost all cases, the struggle pays off and the strategic message development group discovers that it can express a lot in a few words—words that they can remember, words that listeners can understand and will respond to, words that capture the listeners' attention so that more information can be delivered.

Flexible Words, Inflexible Concepts

One of the strengths of a strategic message is that its wording can be adapted to the medium or the situation in which it is being used. Individuals can adapt the language to accommodate relevant factors such as personal style (formal, casual, folksy), the medium (conversation, public speaking, writing), and the occasion (grassroots conclave, board of directors meeting, fundraising pitch). For example, one speaker might use the word *farsighted* while another prefers the term *visionary.* In one situation a writer might use the term *trustworthy* and in another the phrase *practice what we preach.* The value of having a specifically worded message, even though it can be linguistically adapted, is that the words are there to fall back on if needed. The purpose of specific language is to provide a safety net, not verbal handcuffs.

Although there is flexibility in the words used to deliver the strategic message, there is no flexibility in the major points of the message. They must remain the same. The key points are, after all, what the struggle of creating the strategic message was about. They reflect the audience's desire with which the strategic message tries to connect. The concepts of a message do not change, even when the words may.

Summary

- The key to a successful strategic message is conveying it in such a way that your audience can take it in.

- It requires writing and speaking from their perspective, not yours.

- It requires using words that are familiar, not jargon.

- It requires limiting the number of words you use: no more than twenty-five to thirty in a core message.

- It also requires limiting the number of different points you make: no more than three in the core message and in each subset message.

Discussion Questions

1. Is our message focused on what we feel we need to tell our audiences or on what they want to hear?

2. Have we used language that our audience will easily understand?

3. Have we used jargon in our message? If so, is it only because the audience will respond more favorably to the jargon than to more common terms?

4. Have we created a core message that is no longer than thirty words? Is each of our subset messages similarly brief?

5. Have we limited ourselves to no more than three points in our core message and in each of our subset messages?

6. When we speak the messages out loud, do we stumble or are they easy to say?

9. *Putting the Steps Together*
The Process of Message Development

ONCE YOU KNOW the steps, it's time to dance.

Putting the five steps of strategic message development together to create an effective message is like putting steps together to dance a ballet. You need the right people. You need the right space. You need a choreographer.

Over the years, I have developed and refined "the dance" for creating strategic messages. The method works well regardless of the size of the organization, the focus of the message, or the professional background of those involved. It has worked with a small, local teen-pregnancy program wanting greater foundation funding. It has worked with a 100,000-member professional association trying to introduce a best practice. It has even worked with a nationwide firm of six thousand tax experts that wanted greater internal awareness of its knowledge management unit.

The key elements of the method are the message team, the location and logistics of the development meetings, and the facilitator.

The Message Development Team

The strategic message development team is a critical aspect of the development process. Care must always be taken in selecting members because the quality of the team will determine the quality of the message. In many cases, the diversity of the team may be important; as noted earlier, an interdisciplinary team is much more likely to craft messages broad enough to serve the interests of all departments of an organization. Also, people are more likely to use something that they have helped create, or that someone like them has helped create (such as someone in their department or someone with similar expertise). In most cases, the choice of team members also signals the relative importance of the message to those who will use it; if top leaders are involved, people are more likely to use the message than if it is created at a lower level.

For those reasons, these are key considerations in forming a strategic message development team:

- The team should include leaders at the level where the strategic message is going to be used. If the whole organization is going to use the message (which is usually the situation), then top leadership is involved in creating the message, and often a board member or two are involved.

- It must include staff from multiple functional areas, unless only one area is going to use the strategic message—which is highly unusual.

- It should *not* be comprised solely of communications (or marketing or development) staff.

- It should include people whose brains work in a variety of ways—for example, some strategic and some tactical thinkers, not all "creative" types.

- It must involve people who are both decisive and collaborative. The team members need to be strong enough personalities to fully express their viewpoints but flexible enough to be able to find middle ground. Message development may be almost impossible if there are team members who refuse to budge from their perspective.

The optimal size for a strategic message development team is six to nine people. It can be done with fewer, but not fewer than four. It can be done with more, but once the group gets too large, additional time is needed to complete the process because there are simply more people contributing. Internal political considerations may require the team to include certain people, but guard against being so inclusive that the group's creativity is sapped by the process taking too long.

A critical feature of the team is that once the process has started, people can leave the team but no one can join. It is best if people do not leave the process, but there may be situations where someone's schedule permits only limited participation. However, individuals absolutely cannot join the process once it has started. Doing so results in the repetition of discussion and decision making that drags down other participants and weakens the product. Doing so also usually means that someone is participating who is not operating with the same knowledge and understanding as others and whose contributions, therefore, may be off the mark.

Logistics, Facilitator, and Meetings

The logistics of developing a strategic message are similar to the logistics of developing a strategic plan, although a message is created over a period of weeks—not months, as a plan is.

The best process involves three meetings, at least two of which are day-long. Meeting planners should think of the meetings as they think of retreats, and standard retreat logistics should be carefully attended to. The meetings must be held in a location segregated from everyday office activity, and off-site locations should be used if possible. Use of cell phones, PDAs, and other distractions during the meeting times must be prohibited; people can use these during breaks but not during the meeting time. The creature comforts that enhance or impede retreat functioning should be addressed: normal temperature, enough water, and lots of chocolate at three o'clock. Seating should accommodate easy discussion among all participants; horseshoe arrangements usually work best for dialogue and facilitation, while long tables or classroom-style setups tend to inhibit both.

A facilitator, whether paid or volunteer, is essential to the strategic message development process. The team itself needs to spend all of its mental energy thinking about the issues being decided. It should be left to a nonparticipant to guide the work, capture the key ideas that are emerging, and integrate viewpoints into cohesive strains of thought—as well as monitor whether the group needs a break. Moreover, a skilled facilitator can help the group move back and forth through the steps of the process; as a creative exercise, strategic message development does not progress in lockstep fashion for every group but rather flows in one direction, gets interrupted, returns to where it was and resumes discussion, then flows off again. It is the facilitator's job to sense when to let the flow happen and when to assert discipline so that the group maintains focus and makes a decision.

The best facilitator for strategic message development is one who is not only skilled as a facilitator but also a skilled writer. At various points in the process, the facilitator will be saying back to the group what she hears it saying—usually by writing it on flip-chart pages. If the facilitator is not also a writer, then someone else who is a nonparticipant—another "honest broker" of the group's ideas—must be involved and periodically feed back possible message language to the group. Facilitators and scribes are not counted when determining the size of the team.

The work schedule

Depending on the schedule of the team members, the process of developing a strategic message can take anywhere between four and twelve weeks. Generally, it takes four to five weeks when all participants are all local and six to twelve weeks when some must come in from out of town. It is important to create the strategic message in a concentrated period of time so that participants can recall discussions over the course of the process.

Meeting one

The first meeting lasts approximately six to eight hours, and most strategic message development teams work through steps one and two and part of steps three and four. This meeting usually involves the most difficult decision making because it requires the team to identify the action that the organization wants to effect as a result of its strategic message. As was noted in earlier chapters, identifying the action that an organization wants to prompt is difficult, frustrating, and often results in acrimonious discussion.

Specific action is, simply, not a common focus for many nonprofits, foundations, and associations. For this reason, team members will quickly slip into a discussion of increasing awareness or of mission—conversations with which they are more familiar. Participants need to be pressed to keep the conversation directed at identifying the action. Inevitably, some will assert that a single action cannot be identified. With enough facilitation, however, the team will come to identify the essential action that it seeks.

Very often, it takes the strategic message development team three to four hours to make the decision about what action is the goal of the strategic message. In the course of the conversation, team members usually begin identifying potential target audiences and may even begin discussing what motivates those audiences. *Well, if that is going to be the action we want, we'll need to get X or Y group involved,* one participant will say. *How can we,* another will respond, *when we don't provide anything they want.* In this way, the work of one step of the process flows into another step. It is worthwhile to capture speculation about potential audiences on a piece of flip-chart paper, but the group must make a decision about the action before turning its full attention to identifying its target audiences.

Once the action has been determined, the team begins step two: identifying those who must do something for the action to occur. The actors cluster into target audiences. Naming the audiences may lead the team into a side conversation about whether the organization has the capacity to reach one or another audience. Such conversation is important because it anticipates step four, which is when the organization determines whether it is willing to do what is needed to connect with the actors who can help achieve the result the organization wants. Step two is not the time for the group to discuss precisely what changes it would make to connect with new audiences, but it is important for the organization to recognize here that some change may be implicit in its decision to select certain audiences.

Usually the first meeting ends while the group is partway in its step three conversation: identifying the desires of target audiences. It is important, in the process of identifying what will motivate actors to act, to recognize that the motivating desires may have nothing to do with the specific action. For example, a news reporter wants a story exclusively and immediately regardless of whether its subject is the city's homeless people or its art museum. A volunteer may want an opportunity that puts him in contact with others his age regardless of whether he is clearing the Appalachian Trail or assisting at the free clinic. In this discussion, it is important to remember why people do what they do; as hardware store owners know, people buy picture hooks because they want to hang pictures, not because they want picture hooks.

At the end of the first meeting, the team may be anxious and frustrated. People may feel that much has been surfaced but little resolved, and they'll be correct because that is simply where they are in the development process. A lot of creative thought has occurred and been vigorously discussed; if that process has not produced angst, then people probably have not been challenging themselves sufficiently.

The first meeting interlude

Between the first and second meetings, the facilitator (or another designated individual) drafts a core message. This is the only activity that must happen before the next meeting. It may also be possible to draft some of the subset messages for each audience; if so, a draft message matrix is created, showing which subset messages serve which audiences. (See page 17 for a sample message matrix.) The ability to draft subset messages at this point depends on how far the group got in discussing audience desires.

Two other activities may take place during this interlude between meetings. The team may formally or informally test its assumptions about audience desires. Rarely, a group may decide that it needs to interrupt the message development process to undertake a major market research effort like surveying its membership. It is usually impossible to anticipate, at the beginning of the process, whether extensive audience research will be needed because the audiences are not identified until the process has started. Usually, the organization is familiar enough with the proposed audiences that the constellation of their desires is fairly well known. The other activity that may occur, if relevant, is that the organizational leaders begin to think about how willing they are to make the changes needed to meet the desires of certain audiences. No firm decisions are usually made, but leaders begin to think about the capacity and resources needed to meet audience desires, and they develop a sense of the organization's willingness to make changes.

Identifying Desire

How do we know if we identified audience desire correctly?

Every strategic message development team worries about that question. The short answer is, you don't. However, remember that even your audience does not always know what it desires, or wouldn't tell you if you asked.

In reality, most organizations know a great deal about the desires of their target audiences. In almost all cases, most of the audiences are groups they work with frequently, if not constantly. It is rare to have more than one target audience with which the organization is unfamiliar.

Moreover, as an organization heads into strategic message development (or, as stated earlier, between meetings one and two), it can initiate or step up efforts to identify or validate the desires of groups that will most likely be target audiences. For example, if the Family Crisis Center is initiating a job placement program that will need volunteers, it may precede strategic message development with a formal or informal effort to glean information from current volunteers that will help it identify what aspects of the new program might be attractive to volunteers. If resources are available, an organization may undertake traditional market research—such as focus groups or surveys—to garner more information about the desires of audiences that it can clearly anticipate will be targeted. Data gathering need not be expensive; often the best way of knowing what your audiences want is to have a varied array of intentional activities, continually practiced, that are designed to allow you to "hear" them.

In the end, one of the best insurance policies for addressing audience desires correctly is the fact that there are usually three subset messages for each target audience. A group may find that two of the subset messages are more effective than the third; that may indicate that the audience desire at the heart of the third message is incorrectly identified. (It could just as easily mean other things, however, such as language that is less compelling.)

Meeting two

The second meeting, which again is an all-day session, takes final action on steps one and two, and continues or undertakes discussion related to steps three, four, and five. That is, the meeting confirms or changes the action that the message is intended to prompt and who the actors—or target audiences—are who must be activated. Once these decisions are made, it focuses on the work of further identifying the audiences' desires, clustering audiences into groups based on common desire, ascertaining the overlap between the audiences' desires and what the organization is willing to do, and how to word the actual core and subset messages.

The second meeting begins with the facilitator reading the draft core message. The draft message is not circulated prior to the meeting or prior to the reading. This is because in the real world, audiences are more likely to hear messages than read them (and they "hear" in their head even when they read). Therefore, the messages should be easy on the ear. The best way to test that is to hear the words before reading them.

Once read, the draft of the core message is discussed and revised before discussion begins on the subset messages. (The revisions are probably not final. At the end of the day, the core message is revisited to determine whether additional changes need to be made as a result of greater understanding that has developed during discussion of subset messages for each target audience.) The discussion of the core message includes revisiting steps one and two: has the group chosen the action it truly desires and the actors who must be set in motion? When the core message discussion has ended, the facilitator reads any of the subset messages that may have been drafted as a result of the discussion in the first meeting. Again, these are read to the group before being distributed. If no subset messages have been drafted, the group plunges into discussion of the desires of the target audiences.

Discussion of the core and subset messages engages the group in implicit or explicit step four decision making: if we deliver what our audiences want, will the action we want be achieved? The team may make this decision implicitly, by forging ahead with conversation about the messages, or it may make the decision explicitly; if explicit decision making occurs it is usually only in relation to one audience because only one may be so far outside the arena of current operations that serving it would require changes in the organization's allocation of time, money, staff, or other resources.

The discussion also engages the group in step five: creating the strategic message language. As the group discusses the core or subset messages, it inevitably suggests different wording. Words and phrases are tossed out. One group member agrees, another disagrees, someone else offers different wording. One person argues that a term is jargon, another insists that jargon is needed with this audience. Whoever is capturing the words and phrases—whether the facilitator or another—is filling pages of flip-chart paper with suggestions. Often, a complete message or two may fall out of the discussion, but usually all of it is fodder for the message drafter to take away at the end of the day to use in creating the subset messages for each audience.

If the core message was not approved at the beginning of the meeting, the team will return to it at the end of the afternoon, tweak it, and approve it. It is rare that the core message is not complete at the end of the second meeting.

The second meeting interlude

Between the second and third meeting, the message drafter crafts new message language to present at the third meeting. If a message matrix has not been created previously, it is created at this point. Almost always, the core message and perhaps some of the subset messages for each audience have been finalized at the second meeting. All that remains is for the group to discuss and decide the remaining subset messages.

Meeting three

The third meeting begins with the facilitator reading, out loud, the draft messages. Again, no messages are circulated in writing before they are read. Once the messages are read, however, they are distributed in the form of a message matrix. The length of the third meeting varies depending on how much progress was made in the second meeting and how much time has elapsed between the two meetings. If only a few weeks have elapsed, the third meeting will be shorter than if a month or more has passed. Usually, the last meeting takes half a day, although a few groups have completed the work in ninety minutes.

The format for the third meeting is first to read all the subset messages for all audiences. (The core message and all subset messages are read for one audience, then the core message again and the subset messages for another audience, and so on.) Then each audience's messages are individually addressed, discussed, edited, and finalized. In most instances, this discussion tends to be shorter than in previous meetings because there has been so much discussion already about audiences, desires, and appropriate language that common perspectives have evolved.

At the end of the final meeting, it is good to remind the team that a final message matrix will be distributed that contains the core message and all audience subset messages. It is also helpful to remind the team that the messages' language can be adapted depending on the formality of the occasion, the delivery vehicle, and an individual's style, but the *content* of the messages must remain the same.

Using the messages

Although the core message should become easily remembered over time, the various subset messages are unlikely to be completely recalled. It is important to capture the energy that strategic message development creates by quickly reproducing the message matrix and distributing it. The strategic message is more likely to be used if the matrix is made available in multiple formats such as in a wallet card, a desktop or 8½ x 11 poster version, an electronic version, and so on. (You can download a message matrix template from the publisher's web site. Visit www.FieldstoneAlliance.org and search for message matrix.) The goal is to have the strategic message easily accessible whenever and wherever participants are supposed to use the statements.

Once the strategic message is complete, someone should review various organizational materials to determine where language should be changed. What materials are examined depends on whether the strategic message was created to support the whole organization or some subset of it, like an individual program. Frequently, changes are needed in a descriptive brochure, on a web site, in a newsletter, in boilerplate language for foundation proposals and news releases, and in many other places. It may be helpful to have someone who was involved in the message development process, but not on the staff, conduct this review; often, a staff member is so close to the materials that he or she is unable to recognize where change should come.

As with any new tool, it is also important for people in the organization to share their experiences using the message. Many will be reluctant to use the message at first, for a variety of reasons including self-consciousness, uncertainty about whether they are using it correctly, reluctance to change, and other factors. They will be more likely to use it if they hear that others are having success with it and hear the multiple situations where it is being used. This is where leadership comes in; organizational leaders should be sharing with their staff, in meetings and elsewhere, examples of how they are using the message. They should also be asking or requiring staff to tell them ways in which they have used the message. Do not assume that strategic messages will be used just because they have been created; managers at every level should actively monitor message use until they feel that is has become part of their staffs' everyday lives.

Summary

- The key elements of a successful message development process are the message team, the location and logistics of the development meetings, and the facilitator.

- Carefully select your strategic message development team. It should include leaders at the level where the strategic message is going to be used, staff from multiple functional areas, both tactical and creative thinkers, and people who are both decisive and collaborative in nature.

- A strong facilitator—whether paid or volunteer—is essential to the strategic message development process: a facilitator who is also a good writer is ideal.

- The best process involves three meetings, at least two of which are day-long. These meetings allow team members to work through the five-step process with time between meetings for a selected member to draft message language.

- Draft messages should always be presented to the message development team verbally before being distributed on paper.

- It is important to capture the energy that strategic message development creates by quickly reproducing the message matrix and distributing it in a variety of formats.

- Managers at every level should actively monitor message use until they feel that is has become part of their staffs' everyday lives.

Discussion Questions

1. Have we created a strategic message development team of between six and nine people?

2. Is the message development team interdisciplinary? Is senior leadership on the team?

3. Have we created an environment where we can work continually without interruption? Are we giving enough time to the message development work?

4. Are we going to use a facilitator so that all team members can participate fully in the discussions?

5. Is the facilitator, or another nonparticipant, capturing the thoughts of the group in writing?

6. Have we asked the facilitator (or, if a separate writer was involved in the meeting, the writer) to draft messages between meetings so that participants can all have fresh ears for the message?

7. Are we waiting until the draft messages are read aloud before we distribute them to the message development team?

10. *A Case Study*
The Power of Strategic Messages

MOST OF THE IMPORTANT aspects of a strategic message can be seen in a case study of the way that the Center for the Study of Social Policy (CSSP), a think tank based in Washington, DC, used strategic messages to help launch a radically different approach to preventing child abuse and neglect.

In 2003, CSSP was ready to go public with a complex new strategy for preventing child abuse and neglect in America, a problem that had seen little improvement in the thirty-five years since it was first recognized. Over the course of a decade, CSSP intended to achieve a dramatic shift in the prevention paradigm: rather than focusing efforts primarily on the judicial system and punishing offenders, it would shift the focus to early childhood care systems and *intercepting* potentially abusive or neglectful situations.

The think tank was promoting a multifaceted strategy that was very difficult to explain, and it had absolutely no direct means of implementing the strategy. Quite the contrary: it was relatively new to working on primary prevention of child abuse and wanted to be heard by specialists who had been working on the issue for decades. CSSP wasn't part of the early childhood system, whose overworked professionals would need to implement the strategy.

Yet within three years, twenty-seven states competed to be among seven chosen to receive technical assistance from CSSP to implement the strategy.

The seven selected states are undertaking a variety of actions to make the new approach integral to their prevention strategy. For example, Wisconsin is fostering new relationships between state and county child welfare agencies and the early childhood professionals in their communities. Arkansas and Missouri are changing licensing requirements for child care centers. Illinois is altering practices for handling abused children so that they go quickly into child care programs that help protect them. Various institutions in New Hampshire are redesigning academic courses or in-service training for early childhood and state child welfare professionals so that frontline workers understand the new approach.

In addition, sixteen other states are implementing similar changes even though they are receiving no direct technical assistance from CSSP. The federal government's Office on Child Abuse and Neglect is supporting the new approach, providing assistance to additional states to implement the strategy and, in 2007, making the approach the centerpiece of its nationwide outreach during Child Abuse Prevention Month. And the organization that privately accredits high-quality child care centers has changed its accreditation standards to include the concepts.

How did it happen? Many factors contributed, of course. The policy designers were brilliant strategists with expert knowledge of the early childhood field. They had sizeable and multiyear funding from a major foundation. They created an approach that was soundly reasoned and based on solid academic research, empirical data, and firsthand observation—and then they invited their partners to help them refine it. They had established relationships with and were respected by leaders in some areas of child welfare and early childhood development.

All of those assets, however, would have done them little good if CSSP had not been able to get busy people to listen to its idea. So as the organization positioned itself to launch the strategy, it obtained help in designing messages that would capture the attention of its target partners long enough to have the time needed to explain the approach. The organization's leaders knew that, in today's oversaturated communications environment, they wouldn't get the opportunity to talk for an hour about their new model if they couldn't hold their audiences' attention for that fateful first minute.

The strategic messages that CSSP developed were not perfect—few, if any, messages are. The organization struggled to keep the messages short and limit the number of points made. Despite the imperfections, CSSP believes the strategic messages helped it achieve its goals. Its experience demonstrates when strategic messages can be helpful, how the process works, and how messages can change as goals are achieved and new goals set down.

The Situation

Since the late 1960s, when child abuse and neglect were first recognized as problems in the United States, the dominant strategy for addressing them was to arrest the abuser and remove the child from the home. That strategy did little, over the ensuing four decades, to permanently reduce the rate of abuse and neglect. Other prevention strategies, such as home visits and family resource centers, had only limited impact.

CSSP thought a better strategy might be to focus on how early childhood centers could play a role in preventing familial abuse and neglect. Its goal was to determine whether these programs could deliver a more effective method for preventing child abuse and neglect, which threatens an estimated 2.8 million children annually in the United States. It enlisted funding from the Doris Duke Charitable Foundation to underwrite two years of study and strategy development beginning in the fall of 2001.

CSSP first conducted an exhaustive review of academic research on child abuse prevention dating back to the late 1960s. It then convened a panel of nationally known experts to help create the new prevention strategy. The approach focused on building competency within families and children so that situations that might otherwise lead to abuse or neglect did not result in either; at the heart of the approach were five protective factors that, when developed in early childhood care programs, appeared to result in less abuse and neglect. Finally, it conducted a nationwide search for exemplary early childhood care programs that were currently building such competency. It identified twenty-one exemplary centers whose programs, in various ways, built the kind of resiliency in parents and children that might protect against abusive or neglectful episodes. The centers had not designed their programs to prevent child abuse and neglect, yet the result of their programs was a lower incidence of abuse and neglect in their populations than might have been expected.

At the end of two years, CSSP had developed a strategy and could show twenty-one early child care centers around the country where some aspect of the strategy was being played out every day. CSSP not only had a new theoretical approach, it had many places where it could demonstrate that the approach was being implemented using practices that could be replicated elsewhere with minimal changes in programs and staff and minor increases in expenditures. With continued funding from the Doris Duke Charitable Foundation, it was ready to undertake radical change.

Center for the Study of Social Policy's First Message Development

CSSP was in a powerful position as it launched the new strategy, which in essence was the launch of a new movement to prevent child abuse and neglect. The approach was based on sound research, designed by experts, grounded in daily use around the country, and funded by a major foundation.

However, CSSP also faced a daunting challenge: the complexity of the concept and the language used to explain it.

First, the new prevention approach differed radically from the existing one:

- It was based in the early childhood education system, not the government's child welfare and judicial systems.

- It focused on building protection for children within their homes and communities, not only on identifying risks in those areas.

- It sought to overcome or mitigate manageable individual causes of neglect and abuse—such as family crises, parental isolation, and lack of knowledge about child development—rather than removing children from their homes.

Second, CSSP was targeting audiences that used different terms when talking about protecting children. Early childhood professionals talked about building protective factors in families. Child welfare workers talked about moving from being risk-based to being strength-based in its prevention strategy. The focus was similar but the words were quite different. CSSP needed to bridge the jargon divide.

CSSP contracted with a consultant to help it develop a strategic message. Subsequently, it realized that it needed a second message and then a third. As it moved outward in concentric circles from the initial corps of supporters, it discovered that some elements of its existing message remained effective with new audiences and some needed to change.

As it approached the creation of its first strategic message, CSSP fully realized the position it was in. As policy developers, not frontline child care or child abuse prevention professionals, CSSP could do nothing directly to implement its strategy. To achieve the action it desired—implementation—it needed to enlist and activate partners: child care practitioners, state early childhood and child welfare agencies, and child abuse and prevention activist groups. The first step in enlisting these professionals, CSSP decided, was to persuade the leadership of those communities to get on board with the idea. The chart on the next page, CSSP's First Message Development Steps, illustrates how the organization created its first strategic message.

CSSP's First Message Development Steps

STEP ONE: Action Identification	The Center for the Study of Social Policy (CSSP) wanted key national leaders to join it in refining the new prevention approach and promoting it with their colleagues.
STEP TWO: Audience Identification	To achieve permanent change, CSSP knew it needed the active participation of three groups: child care practitioners, state early childhood and child welfare agencies, and child abuse and neglect prevention activist groups. To reach those groups, it needed first to enlist each group's national leaders. These key leaders—only about a dozen individuals—were the audience for CSSP's first strategic message.
STEP THREE: Identification of Audience Desires	CSSP knew that these leaders wanted a more effective way of protecting children from abuse and neglect. They also knew that the leaders would not quickly jump at a radically new approach and find resources to implement it. CSSP identified three desires that would need to be met to gain their involvement: (1) a better strategy for preventing abuse and neglect that was based on sound research plus practical application, (2) participation in refining that strategy, and (3) money to support their participation.
STEP FOUR: Identification of Overlap with CSSP's Desires	CSSP believed that the leaders' desires overlapped with CSSP's, and that CSSP could meet those desires in this way: 1. Its new approach was based on well-respected research by academic experts and was being demonstrated in exemplary child care centers already. 2 It was willing to work with the leaders to figure out the best ways of implementing the strategy—in programs and through policy—wherever reasonable opportunity presented itself. 3. It had funds available to provide technical assistance that each partner would need to undertake implementation.
STEP FIVE: Message Creation	CSSP created a core message and subset messages. The subset messages were, with one exception, identical for each target audience (which is unusual in message development). What made it possible was the tiny size of the total target audience—about a dozen people (which is also extremely rare).

Message Matrix 1, below, shows the core and subset messages that CSSP developed.

Message Matrix 1

Core Message
With funding from the Doris Duke Foundation, CSSP has developed a promising new strategy for preventing child abuse and neglect that builds on the assets of early childhood care and education.

Subset Message 1
We want you to partner with us in developing, refining, and implementing this strategy.

Subset Message 2
We are optimistic that we will get additional resources from funders to develop and implement this breakthrough strategy with our partners.

Subset Message 3
There are important actions that we urge you to take now. Your action will signal to funders that you are willing to partner in developing the strategy, and this will help increase the likelihood of broad funder support. [This point was further developed with specific actions that varied depending on the specific target audience.]

Center for the Study of Social Policy's Second Message Development

Within two months, the Center for the Study of Social Policy succeeded in enlisting key national leaders, opening the door to make its vision become reality. For example, it joined forces with the National Association for the Education of Young Children, the 100,000-member professional association of early childhood educators. It enlisted the National Alliance of Children's Trust and Prevention Funds, which provides financial support to local child abuse prevention programs in all fifty states. It created a network of the twenty-one exemplary child care centers. It won the involvement of government officials such as the director of child care and parent services in Georgia and a regional director of the U.S. Department of Health and Human Services in Texas.

It then began to focus on how to enlist the "troops behind the generals"— that is, the frontline professionals whose actions would need to change to implement the new strategy. This new goal brought new challenges, and among them was the need to develop a fresh message. While the target audience for CSSP's first strategic message had been a mere handful of people, now the organization would target thousands. Although the size changed dramatically, the process for deciding what to say remained the same.

The chart on pages 115–116, CSSP's Second Message Development Steps, shows how CSSP worked through the message development steps to create its second strategic message.

The chart on page 117, Message Matrix 2, shows the second message that was created.

CSSP's Second Message Development Steps

STEP ONE: Action Identification	The Center for the Study of Social Policy wanted the new approach to start being used throughout the country.
STEP TWO: Audience Identification	CSSP reaffirmed its target audiences: • Early childhood professional organizations, because early childhood professionals were the implementers of the strategy. • Child abuse and neglect prevention organizations, because they had experience with practical methods and public policies for reducing abuse and had advocates in cities and states across the country who presumably would be willing to support an effective new approach. • Government early childhood and agencies, because they could change policies in ways that could have a wholesale impact on the adoption of a new approach.
STEP THREE: Identification of Audience Desires	In various ways, including talking with the leadership in each audience segment and relying on one sector's survey of professionals, CSSP identified what desires each group had for a new approach to abuse and neglect prevention. All three groups wanted a *doable* solution, not a remedy disconnected from the real world. In an industry strained by overwork and low funding, early childhood professionals also wanted one that could be implemented at minimal cost in time and money. Child abuse and neglect prevention organizations wanted one that would have abuse and neglect cases resolved somewhere outside the punitive judicial system. They also wanted prevention efforts to become mainstream, rather than be actions only focused on aberrant or "other" people. Government early childhood agencies wanted better outcomes for children, and child welfare agencies wanted a solution that would keep children out of the welfare system.

(*continued*)

STEP FOUR: Identification of Overlap with CSSP's Desires	CSSP knew that its approach could meet the desires of each group. The practices were already being used in child care centers, proving that the approach was doable. Almost all of the methods were low cost and were being implemented by hard-working child care professionals. The CSSP approach moved prevention efforts out of the judicial sphere; basing primary prevention in child care centers definitely made the issue more mainstream—helping everyone, not just aberrant individuals or families. And, by having an approach that relied on recognizing potentially abusive or neglectful situations and moving to remediate them before harm occurred, chances increased that families would be kept out of crisis and off welfare.
STEP FIVE: Message Creation	CSSP made two interesting language decisions in crafting the core and subset messages:

1. Instead of the terms *abuse* and *neglect,* the phrase *harm to children* was used in the core message because it was believed that preschool teachers might more easily hear that phrase and remain open to the remainder of the message. Consistent with the flexibility of a strategic message, those delivering the message could instead use the phrase *child abuse and neglect* if they felt it would be more successful in a given situation.

2. CSSP used jargon—evidence-based, resilience building framework—in two subset messages. Message designers believed that those audiences would understand the language and respond positively to the wording and the content of the phrase.

Message Matrix 2

Core Message		
Small but significant changes in early childhood programs offer an effective new strategy for supporting parents under stress and preventing harm to children.		
Subset Message: Early Childhood Professionals	**Subset Message:** Child Abuse and Neglect Prevention Organizations	**Subset Message:** Government Child Welfare and Early Childhood Agencies
This new strategy will enable early childhood professionals to respond quickly and effectively to help families who are struggling and children who are at risk of long-term harm or who have challenging behaviors.	This strategy brings child abuse and neglect prevention into the mainstream and is an opportunity we can't afford to miss.	Investing in this early childhood approach will keep children out of the system by reaching families at risk before they come into contact with it.
Any program can make the necessary changes to implement this strategy with a small investment in resources and planning.	This provides a new opportunity to plug into an existing normative system with a strong existing infrastructure, and it exponentially extends the reach of prevention services.	We are interested in working with states that want to pilot a partnership between child welfare agencies and early childhood programs to support young children in the system.
This offers an opportunity for forming new partnerships and bringing additional resources and a new constituency to support the work that early childhood programs do with parents.	This strategy comes from an evidence-based, resilience building framework that offers a new way of thinking about child abuse and neglect prevention.	This strategy comes from an evidence-based, resilience-building framework that offers a new way of thinking about child abuse and neglect prevention.

Center for the Study of Social Policy's Third Message Development

While working at the national level, the Center for the Study of Social Policy was also working with twenty-one exemplary early childhood care centers to develop the nuts-and-bolts application of its approach. The centers, now armed with an understanding of how some of their long-standing practices could help prevent child abuse, were able to help CSSP and early adopters of the methods better understand how to apply the strategy.

As the embodiment of the approach, these twenty-one childcare centers would be educating other important audiences about the new strategy—its value, its methods, and its challenges. At one point or another, leaders from the twenty-one early childhood care centers might talk to people in their community or state who could in some way advance the new approach more broadly: policymakers, funders, licensing agencies, regulatory agencies, grassroots activists, reporters, and directors of other child care centers. It was important that leaders from the twenty-one exemplary centers presented the strategic message consistently with the way other advocates of the CSSP approach talked about it. For that reason, CSSP wanted them to have language that positioned the new approach to child abuse and neglect prevention consistently.

Moreover, as the embodiment of best practices in the field, the twenty-one centers represented a valuable asset that CSSP wanted to protect and, if possible, strengthen. One way to do that was to give the centers language that helped them promote their excellence with important stakeholders: internal audiences such as staff and parents and external audiences such as funders and community leaders. Giving the twenty-one centers language that helped them legitimately claim their place as exemplary and innovative centers was also a way for CSSP to repay them for the help they provided in moving the idea forward. (Note that this win-win situation is an outcome of strategic message development, which happens at the intersection of the organization's desires and the audiences' desires.)

How CSSP Used the Strategic Message

The core message that the Center for the Study of Social Policy developed in 2003 is still being used today. In the intervening years, the core message and elements of subset messages have appeared in a wide variety of CSSP communications. The strategic message has also been picked up and used by some of the child care centers, community activists, state government agencies, and other organizations that are partnering with CSSP to execute the strategy nationwide.

These are some of the places where CSSP used its messages:

- Descriptive brochure
- Conference speeches
- Training materials
- Requests for proposals for pilot state participation
- Grant proposals for funders
- Meetings with policymakers
- Meetings with community-based activist groups
- Presentations to state agencies
- Business letters
- Its web site
- Conversations with potential partner organizations

Just weeks before a meeting that drew the twenty-one center directors together from across the country, CSSP recognized the value of having a strategic message for them to use. However, the crush of work leading up to the meeting meant that there was not time to engage in as deliberative a process as had been used the first two times. However, familiarity with the principles from its prior two experiences helped CSSP move quickly to seize the opportunity it saw. The chart on page 120 shows how CSSP quickly moved through the five steps.

CSSP's Third Message Development Steps

STEP ONE: Action Identification	CSSP wanted each of the twenty-one centers to help maintain or increase public and private support for the new approach and to present the new strategy consistently with the way the rest of the CSSP-managed campaign was presented.
STEP TWO: Audience Identification	CSSP was developing this message for the twenty-one centers, so the target audiences were the centers' audiences, not CSSP's audiences. It knew that these audiences were central to the support base of each child care center: staff, parents, funders, and community leaders and activists in various areas.
STEP THREE: Identification of Audience Desires	CSSP recognized that each of the twenty-one centers' audiences would have different reasons—desires—for knowing about the center's exemplary status: • Center staff wanted to be associated with a high-quality center. • Parents wanted their child to attend a high-quality center and one that saw supporting parents as an integral part of its operations. • Funders wanted to support a high-quality operation or to support cutting-edge innovations in social services. • Community leaders wanted to know about a new way of reducing the child abuse and neglect.
STEP FOUR: Identification of Overlap with CSSP's Desires	CSSP knew that its approach, which was reflected to some degree in the work of each center, met the desire of each of these groups.
STEP FIVE: Message Creation	CSSP decided that the core message it created for early childhood professionals, welfare agency officials, and abuse and neglect activists needed only slight alteration to work for the child care centers. This minimal alteration meant that there would be greater consistency of message. The subset messages needed to be created from scratch, however, because those groups had not been audiences for previous messages.

It was highly unusual that CSSP developed a strategic message for another entity (the child care centers) to deliver. One of the central tenets of strategic message development is that *those who will deliver the message are intimately involved in the creative process.* In this regard, the third CSSP message development experience ran contrary to an important principle. Nevertheless, CSSP believed that it was advancing toward its goal by providing this message matrix to the twenty-one centers for their use:

Message Matrix 3 (for the twenty-one exemplary centers)

Core Message			
Our center is part of a nationwide network of early childhood professionals that is exploring how small but significant changes in programs can provide an effective new strategy for supporting parents under stress and preventing harm to children.			
Subset Messages: Staff	**Subset Messages:** Parents	**Subset Messages:** Funders	**Subset Messages:** Community Leaders
Although we are picking up new ideas from the network, most of the preventive work that occurs here flows from things we are already doing. Our current work, in fact, is why we have been selected as one of twenty-one exemplary centers that make up this network.	We have always believed that helping our children meant helping their families understand them better and giving support to those families during stressful times. Experts now think that this approach also protects children from maltreatment.	This is the first major change in the strategy for preventing child abuse and neglect in decades—and the first to base prevention not in the government system but in the early childhood system.	This network is the leading edge of a new strategy for preventing child abuse and neglect—the first new strategy in decades. Instead of being based in the government system, as is currently the case, the new strategy is based in the early childhood system.

(continued)

Subset Messages: Staff (*continued*)	**Subset Messages:** Parents (*continued*)	**Subset Messages:** Funders (*continued*)	**Subset Messages:** Community Leaders (*continued*)
What national experts are recognizing is that work such as we do to build a child's social and emotional development, create relationships with families, and help families that are struggling actually helps prevent child abuse and neglect also.	We haven't designed our program specifically to protect children against abuse and neglect, but experts now tell us that many of the things we do have that as one of their results.	The core of the strategy is a framework of five protective factors that was developed with involvement from leading academics, child welfare policymakers, and early childhood practitioners from around the country.	National experts are now recognizing that the way programs like ours approach early childhood education—building a child's social and emotional development, creating relationships with families, and helping families that are struggling—actually helps prevent child abuse and neglect also.
As we continue to strengthen our program, we will be conscious of ways in which current program elements and program improvements may help protect our children from maltreatment.	We are proud that we were one of twenty-one places in the country identified as having a program that supports our working as a team with parents and families to help our children develop in healthy ways.	We are involved because a nationwide search identified us as one of twenty-one exemplary early childhood centers whose current programming and staffing contain elements that build those five protective factors.	We are involved because a nationwide search identified us as one of twenty-one exemplary early childhood centers whose current programming and staffing contain elements that build protection against child maltreatment.

Strategic Messages and Social Movements

The Center for the Study of Social Policy case study demonstrates that a strategic message can be developed to support individual outreach, broad policy change, or even a nascent national movement. So when is a strategic message a "people-mover" and when it is a "mountain-mover?"

As the case study reveals, some of CSSP's strategic messages are intended to change the behavior of individuals and some are intended to modify the behavior of large groups. Ultimately, CSSP wants to transform the behavior of a whole society.

As CSSP works around the country to advance its new approach, its strategic message must compel the action of individuals willing to change how their communities protect children from abuse and neglect. In some places, CSSP works with individual child care center directors who model the approach for other centers. In other places, it works with college professors who alter what teachers learn. In others, it works with social service directors who press to reform government systems that address prevention.

At the same time, CSSP is working to change the behavior of national groups. As it is at the state and local level, CSSP is meeting with some success nationally. A key agency of the federal government is helping advance the new approach. The professional association that accredits top-quality child care centers has incorporated the approach into its new accreditation standards.

At both levels, CSSP still delivers its core message: *small but significant changes in programming and staffing of early childhood programs offer an effective new strategy for supporting parents under stress and preventing harm to children.*

Is this the message of an increasingly widespread social experiment? Or is it the message of a new social movement?

No one knows the answer, of course. No one can see a tipping point at the moment it is reached. Who can say when the effort to stop smoking ceased being based on smokers' rights and became a movement to protect nonsmokers? Or when the battle against drunk driving became more about promoting designated drivers than locking up drunk ones?

(continued)

There is a good chance that, one day, American society will consider it obvious that the best way to prevent child abuse is to help families stay out of crises that may result in abuse or neglect, and that the best people to identify risky situations are the child care professionals who see the children and families every day. At that point, one could say that what was once a message aimed at individuals and groups evolved into the message of a national movement.

Summary

Judy Langford, CSSP's project director, calls the strategic messages a significant factor in helping move the radical new approach from concept to implementation. She notes that few of the ideas and little of the research data underlying the approach are new.

"It was the unique way we presented the ideas that made all the difference," she says. "People could finally hear what we were saying when they saw their own practices and ideas embedded in our messages. Advocates and practitioners from very different spheres have used the same language to develop new ways of working together, and the enthusiasm has been infectious."

As with most strategic messages, it is impossible to prove the direct contribution of any of these messages. Inference is a better method and, inferentially, the messages were successful:

- The first core message—targeted at a handful of national leaders—helped CSSP connect with leaders and get them on board quickly.

- The second core message has been used since 2003—a good sign that it is doing its job. In addition, in 2004 when CSSP sought a few states to be pilot sites for wide implementation of the strategy, it feared that it might fail to get even three or four to apply because of the complexity of the strategy and the radical paradigm shift. However, twenty-seven states applied and the federal government and the field's primary professional association also took significant steps to advance the strategy. Obviously, numerous factors played a part in this overwhelming response, but one element was the clear way that CSSP could articulate its strategy and its benefits to the target audiences.

• The third message, used by the twenty-one exemplary child care centers, has helped several of them raise additional money (as much as $500,000 for centers in California and Washington, DC) for their work. It has helped centers in Georgia, Michigan, and Illinois get contracts to train early child-hood professionals in the use of the practices. Centers in New Jersey and Georgia have succeeded in getting state officials to introduce elements of the strategy into the statewide pre-kindergarten programs. Again, these accomplishments are due to numerous factors; one of those factors has been the ability of the programs to explain a complex and dramatically new approach to target audiences quickly, clearly, and in a way that con-nects to the audiences' desires.

In 2007, implementation—and continued refinement—of the CSSP ap-proach exceeded its expectations. CSSP was providing direct technical as-sistance to more than twice as many states as it had originally anticipated, and many other states were implementing the approach even without its help. The federal government was getting behind the new strategy. The field's professional association was mandating elements of the approach in centers that receive its highly valued accreditation. It appears that CSSP, in conjunction with innovative leaders in child care, child welfare, and child abuse prevention, may succeed in radically changing the way child abuse and neglect prevention is approached nationwide, with the hope that the new strategy may lead, finally, to a permanent reduction in its incidence.

11. Other Applications of the Strategic Message Framework

BY NOW, MANY LEADERS may have discerned the hidden truth of strategic message development: the Action Connection framework used to develop strategic messages restructures decision making in a manner that can help organizations make other important strategic decisions.

The framework and five-step process explained in this book provide non-profit, foundation, and association leaders with a practical and powerful way to make strategic decisions in many areas of the organization. The simplicity of the process ensures that it can be quickly learned—and applied—by professionals in all departments and at every management level. As a result, strategic thinking happens more often throughout the organization, not just in the president's office. It gives executives the means to analyze and decide strategic issues in a consistent manner, every day, throughout the organization.

Leadership is all about keeping your eye on the ball and getting people to do what you want. The Action Connection framework used for developing strategic messages supports that dual focus, which is why it delivers such high value.

The framework and process help leaders surmount one of the biggest challenges of leadership: simultaneously focusing on *what* the goal is and *how* to activate the people needed to achieve the goal. This is a challenge in any work sector. Military leaders must focus on taking control of a location *and* on leading their troops to capture it. Business leaders must focus on the product being produced *and* on how that product will be marketed. Non-profit leaders must focus on what the organization is doing (programs) *and* on how it is connecting to its major constituencies (marketing). Leadership is all about keeping your eye on the ball and getting people to do what you want. The framework used for developing strategic messages supports that dual focus, which is why it delivers such high value. Specifically, its applications include:

- Filtering new ideas

- Developing programs

- Raising revenue

- Helping executives focus on executive decisions

The Framework as a New Idea Filter

New ideas are like rich chocolate for many dynamic leaders: temptations almost impossible to resist. The homeless shelter's program director wants to add job training to the shelter's portfolio of services. The arts center's volunteer coordinator is urging a novel way of recruiting young volunteers. The professional association's conference director knows her fresh market-ing approach will attract more attendees. The foundation's program officer is certain that an innovative evaluation system will improve grantees' ef-fectiveness. The hospice's development officer has a new idea for raising revenue through cause-related fundraising. Each new day sees a "must-do" idea surface somewhere in the organization.

As an idea filter, the Action Connection framework is a critical reorientation of thinking for most nonprofits— away from why their audience *should* do something and toward what they *want* to do.

While associations and nonprofits rarely lack for good ideas, they often lack a consistent and systematic way of assessing the relevance and potential of each. New ideas commonly sink or swim based on decision making that applies varying standards or is influenced by irrelevant factors such as the popularity of the program area that would house the new project or of the individual who proffers the idea. Innovative proposals become new programs without a stringent assessment of their mission relevance. Ill-conceived new procedures become expensive or ineffective operating practices because there was no careful vetting of their costs and benefits.

The five steps of the strategic message development process, if more widely applied, help organizations and associations avoid these pitfalls. Essentially, they provide a means for filtering ideas, allowing only the best to move forward. This is how each step works as an **idea filter**:

Step One: Action Identification. By focusing an organization on the *action* that it wants to elicit, the Action Connection framework ensures that a new idea—for a program, process, or practice—is vetted rigorously. Those proposing the new approach are forced to articulate the outcome—the action—that they seek by implementing the new idea. Armed with that information, those assessing the idea can then identify how that outcome would advance the organization's mission, operating effectiveness, or other relevant goal. This helps weed out, at an early stage, those "good ideas" that are not really good for a particular organization because they are irrelevant to its mission, inconsistent with its structure, or impossible given its resources.

Step Two: Audience Identification. Through requiring the identification of target audiences, the framework forces decision makers to be clear about what groups must be reached to implement the new program or procedure—such as current staff, stakeholders, new clients, or new donors. Among other things, this forces a group to begin assessing the resource allocation impact of the new proposal: Is the organization currently reaching these audiences? If not, is it willing to direct resources to reach them?

Step Three: Identification of Audience Desire. Here, decision makers must face the acid test of the new idea: is there "anything in it" for their audiences to act as the organization wants? It may be a good idea for the organization, and the organization may be able to reach the audiences it wants, but how will those people respond? Will they say *Yes, we're in* or *Who cares?* This step forces an organization to do what most so rarely do—figure out *why* the people it seeks to activate would be willing to act. This is a critical reorientation of thinking for most nonprofits—away from why their audience *should* do something and toward why it *wants* to do something.

Step Four: Overlapping Desire. If the organization wants something, and determines that its audiences would want it too (even if for different reasons), then the question becomes whether the organization is able or willing to marshal resources to implement the new program, process, or practice. By stopping to assess whether there is any overlap between what the audiences want and what the organization is willing to do, the organization confronts important major resource allocation questions: can we deliver, do we want to deliver, must we give up something else to be able to deliver?

Step Five: Reaching the Audience. The final question is also a resource question: Are we able to reach the people we have targeted and who, we believe, want what we are offering? Do we have the right vehicles for communicating with them? Can we talk in language that moves them to action? In the end, even the best ideas will fail if those taking the actions don't hear about them—or find them compelling.

Many nonprofit leaders are energetic, innovative, and creative—exactly the sort of people for whom new ideas are seductive. New ideas, of course, are often the lifeblood of successful organizations, and inhibiting the forward movement of good ones would be a mistake. However, it would be a gift to inhibit the forward movement of poorly conceived, off-mission, or unachievable ideas—the kind that too often float up to the level of senior staff and even into board meetings. Inhibiting the forward movement of such ideas helps an organization maintain focus and direct its energies productively. Using the Action Connection framework as a filter for new proposals imposes a healthy self-discipline for those tempted by the siren call of the latest bright idea.

The Framework as a Program Development Tool

There are three ways in which the Action Connection framework helps program developers create and critique new initiatives. It narrows the range of ways in which an initiative can be implemented. It keeps designers focused on critical factors as the project is crafted. And, after the program has been operating for a time, it helps evaluators analyze where it might be changed and strengthened.

There are many, many different ways to implement a good idea, and the framework helps program designers pick the best one. The idea-vetting process just described supplies program developers with directives that define parameters within which they work. The purpose of the program has been clarified. The target audiences for the program are known. The desires that will motivate those people have been identified. Instead of fifty good ways to design the program, the universe of possibilities has shrunk to closer to five as a result of the filtering process.

The framework also helps designers stay on track as they fashion the new initiative. All along the way, the questions are the same: have we designed to deliver the action we want? Is the program shaped in a way that gives our target audiences something they want? Are we living within the framework's area of overlap—where *we* will get what we want as well as our audiences getting what they want? The framework helps guard against slipping back into a "me" orientation that is so focused on the organization that its target audiences' desires are ignored. Conversely, it guards against being so audience-focused that the project ends up pleasing a target audience but not achieving the organization's goals.

After the program has been operating for a time, the Action Connection framework helps organizational leaders evaluate it and identify why it succeeded, how it could be strengthened, or whether it should be ended. Was the action sought achieved? Did the organization get what it wanted? Did the action, in the end, turn out to be something it *did* want and that it still wants? Had it correctly identified who could make the action happen, or did it overlook critical actors? Did it understand what its target audiences wanted, or is more work needed there? Did it use its tools for reaching those audiences and use them most effectively? Where did things go right and wrong, and what corrective action will produce greater success?

The Framework as a Revenue Development Tool

Usually, those who must sell the organization, its mission, and its activities quickly recognize the extended value of the framework that is used to develop strategic messages. The job of fundraisers, communicators, and marketers is greatly simplified if their organization uses the Action Connection framework as a decision-making tool. Working through the five steps usually results in marketers being armed with concrete descriptions, targeted action, identified audiences, and language aimed at specific audience desire instead of weak tools like vague sketches, one-size-fits-all actions, and catchy-but-empty phrases.

When an organization defines the specific action that it seeks and can articulate how that action advances its mission, potential donors, clients, or customers readily understand what they are buying. Even if the donor (or customer or client) does not offer support now, there is a good chance that she or he will be impressed with the organization's clarity and be more receptive to overtures in the future. Conversely, when an organization cannot articulate what goal it seeks or how the goal ties to its mission, it is significantly more difficult to sell a prospect now, and it undermines future approaches.

Unambiguous identification of target audience also helps development professionals and other marketers be more efficient and effective in their outreach. The large universe of audiences to which an organization might want to "sell" something—foundations, donors, corporate sponsors, association members, and news reporters—is easier to reduce to manageable size when it is clear *who* the target audiences are and *why* they are the audiences.

For fund development and marketing professionals, the part of the Action Connection framework that focuses on audience desire is like a lifeboat to someone adrift in an ocean. Too often, these specialists are charged with persuading prospects about the value of an organization, program, or idea by colleagues who are stuck in the mind-set of "everything we do is important and people should care." It's like being dropped in the ocean with no clue about which direction to swim to find land. When the framework forces those colleagues to look at their program through the lens of others' desires, they gain a more realistic perspective. That greater understanding can lead to their delving more deeply into the details of their program—its methods and its value. That additional detail can significantly strengthen the development professional's proposal, funding request, or marketing pitch.

The Framework as an Executive Management Tool

The framework used in strategic message development, more broadly used, provides an organization's top executives and board of directors with a systematic approach to decision making that can save time and increase effectiveness and efficiency. By requiring appropriate decision making at lower operational levels, the process frees executive leadership to focus on executive-level decisions. It provides board members with a common approach to addressing issues, which increases the efficient use of board meeting time. Over time, the regular application of the methodology trains all staff to think strategically, which improves decision making when periodic large strategic initiatives are undertaken, such as strategic planning or institutional identity review.

These are a few ways in which the Action Connection framework returns benefits to senior leaders:

Executives focus on executive, not staff, issues. Through the consistent application of the five-step process, the ideas and recommendations that flow from managers to directors to executive leadership are more sharply focused and carefully constructed. An organization or association's most senior decision makers spend their time addressing important strategic and resource allocation issues rather than thinking through good-sounding ideas or redesigning loosely conceived programs.

Board involvement is more meaningful and productive. New proposals that flow from staff to board committees—whether program, development, communications, or management—can be consistently vetted by board members and presented to the full board with a standard approach. Board committees feel their work is more worthwhile, and board meetings have a consistency of presentation that helps members stay focused and involved.

Evaluation of operations is easier. The clear decisions that the framework requires makes it easier to analyze organizational operations and identify whether objectives are being achieved. The clarity also helps determine whether failure to achieve objectives might be due to planning rather than implementation, or vice versa.

Overarching organizational issues have more focus. A variety of overarching issues are easier to address when all areas of the organization are actively contributing information and perspectives about what the organization is doing, for whom, and based on what assumptions of shared desire between the organization and its audiences. For instance, questions related to organizational identity can be addressed based on more information and ongoing consideration, especially if the organization institutionalizes means of obtaining audience feedback on a continual basis. For another example: periodic strategic planning is more vigorous because staff and board are consistently looking at the strategic relevance of programs.

A Framework for Thinking

In 2005, a Northwestern University professor helped develop strategic messages for an organization on whose board of directors he served.[23] Following the first message development meeting, he took the message framework's core concepts back to campus and, in the first week, applied them in three different university settings.

His experience illustrates the dynamic impact that the Action Connection framework can have in circumstances where the objective is not to create a strategic message. The process, he found, simply "gives a framework for thinking about things—a framework that is instantly understood once it is explained, but most people don't naturally think that way so you don't know it until someone points it out."

The process, he noted, is especially useful in an academic setting, which is non-hierarchical (as are many nonprofit organizations) and where people with tenure

(continued)

cannot be coerced into doing what others say. He found that the Action Connection diagram was powerful and useful in a variety of ways: it helped some focus and clarify what they wanted, it helped others identify the desires of those they needed to work with, and for still others it helped them see the overlap between the two that showed where sustained action and meaningful dialogue could occur.

The first instance involved a cross-university initiative in one subject area. "There were a zillion ideas being thrown out, entirely from the point of view of 'it would be neat to do this,'" he explained. "In an academic setting, classes and publications tend to be pushed out from an individual's perspective without a lot of thinking about the receptive side. But when I asked Who is this for? What do they want? What would motivate them? it just changed the discussion and quickly got it focused."

The second instance was a curriculum review committee that had already met twice to discuss changes in the degree requirements for a certain undergraduate major. Although the department was being offered significant additional financial support from the university administration if certain changes were made, the faculty group became bogged down because members disagreed with some of the administration's recommendations. "In the middle of the third meeting, I introduced the Venn diagram image [the Action Connection] because the discussion was in free-fall, really going over a cliff," the professor said. "I used it to refocus discussion on where I was hearing points of commonality between the faculty and the administration. What we found was that 80 percent of what the faculty believed was needed was in that shaded area of overlap with what the administration wanted." The group discovered it was spending 90 percent of its time debating the 20 percent of its desire that was not mirrored in the administration's request. The diagram "forced people to get off nonstarter positions and think in terms of how they could get what they wanted but also respond to what the administration wanted," the professor said.

The last use was with a campus group that wanted to affiliate with a departmental research center. "The Venn diagram gave me a framework for thinking about the proposal. It oriented me away from what resources we could provide to thinking about what they wanted and what I wanted in tangible terms, not just pretty words." Using the Action Connection diagram, he was able to show the campus group where the center's mission and the group's mission fit together and how they could structure an arrangement where they both got things they wanted.

Summary

- The Action Connection framework, used in developing strategic messages, can be used to make important strategic decisions in other operational areas.

- The framework can be used as a filter to ensure that new ideas come before decision makers only after a careful and systematic process that weeds out inadequately prepared proposals.

- The framework can be used to help program planners develop stronger programs and development staff create more powerful proposals.

- The framework can increase the efficiency and effectiveness of decisions made by executive leadership, including the board of directors.

Discussion Questions

1. Are there ways that we could use the Action Connection framework to bring more focus to our decision making in various areas of operations?

2. Would using the framework help us design programs that are clearly defined in their outcomes and more tailored to achieve those outcomes?

3. Would using the framework decrease the time spent researching and writing funding proposals and/or increase the success ratio in our solicitations to foundations, donors, and other funders?

4. If we used the framework as a structure for presenting information to the board of directors, would it improve the board's contribution to the organization by sharpening its discussions and defining the parameters for its decision making?

Conclusion

STRATEGIC MESSAGE DEVELOPMENT today is where strategic planning was in the mid 1980s.

At that time, increasing numbers of new associations and nonprofit groups created resource competition for existing ones. Long-established organizations found themselves struggling to maintain their place in the world. Newer entities began to siphon off funders, volunteers, members, clients, customers, donors, staff, and board members who had once been "theirs." They had to change the way they had always operated or face probable decline.

One of the major ways that organizations succeeded in the new environment was to learn how to plan and execute their operations more strategically. High performance became tied to clear identification of mission, rational strategy, achievable goals, and, later, evaluation.

Now, most nonprofit organizations recognize the need to do strategic planning, know at least some of the techniques, and believe they apply them in their planning at least occasionally. Nonprofit leaders are expected to understand the value of strategic planning. For nonprofit organizations and associations of all sizes, it is considered a standard business practice.

The change did not happen overnight, of course. Leaders recognized the challenge before they identified strategic planning as a key part of the solution. They accepted their need for planning before they understood how to do it. Over the years, however, most successful organizations have learned how to think and act strategically, to a greater or lesser extent.

Today's challenge is more difficult than what faced nonprofits starting in the 1980s. The attention and energy of the audiences that nonprofits consider "theirs" is being sought not merely by other organizations but by virtually every entity in society. The threat is unmistakable and grave: it is increasingly difficult to capture the attention of and connect with individuals whose actions are essential to achieving mission.

Fortunately, a critical part of the solution is beginning to be recognized: strategic message development. Whether in small local nonprofits or large national ones, leaders are recognizing that achieving mission in today's world requires them not just to plan strategically but also to speak strategically.

Unfortunately, the need for strategic messages is more widely recognized than acted on: a foundation-funded survey in 2005 found that almost two-thirds of nonprofit organizations acknowledged that they do not use agreed-upon messages even though they recognize the need for them.[24] Many do not understand what a strategic message is or how to develop such messages. It is time to learn, because the mark of tomorrow's high-achieving nonprofits will be that strategic messaging has become both a mental orientation and a standard business practice.

The mark of tomorrow's high-achieving nonprofits will be that strategic messaging has become both a mental orientation and a standard business practice.

Said another way; using strategic messages needs to become a way of thinking as well as a way of doing. Inherent in a strategic message is a mental framework, not just a five-step process. Tomorrow's top leaders will have a messaging orientation, a lens for viewing situations and a means for addressing them. Ann Cramer, director of IBM corporate community relations and a former member of the national United Way board of directors, has it right when she says that nonprofits need to adopt a strategic mind-set around messages. "You remember when we all got the managing-by-objectives mind-set: mission, vision, goals, objectives—they became a mind-set. And diversity—you enter a room now and you notice whether there are any women, any minorities…that's a mind-set. Nonprofits have to get that kind of mind-set when thinking about messaging."[25]

Acquiring that new mind-set requires most people to think in new ways. That is tough at any time but especially now, when it feels like there is not even time to think in old ways—or to think at all.

For many organizations, however, the biggest impediment to strategic message development may not be the need to think in new ways, but the need to make hard decisions. The term "strategic message development" leads some to believe that the endeavor is primarily a writing challenge, but that is wrong. Capturing the right words is the easy part of message development. What is much harder are the questions and answers that precedes it: *What is it we really want? Who is it we must engage and do we want to engage with them? Can we provide what they want, or are we willing to change so that we can?* More strategic messages fail because of poor thinking and decision making than because of poor expression.

Strategic message development challenges the culture of many associations and nonprofits. It requires an organization to make choices that are often difficult and to articulate them. Choosing one action over another is a challenge when it feels like work needs to be done in so many areas if the organization is going to make a difference. Some nonprofit organizations are reluctant to embrace these tasks because of the discomfort that exists when there is not unanimous support for the decisions. Exposing disagreement is painful in a culture that prides itself on collegiality, inclusively, and fairness. Difficult as these challenges are, clear and considered decision making is a prerequisite for strategic message development.

And, strategic message development is a prerequisite for organizational effectiveness in today's world—and tomorrow's.

Appendix

Organizational Needs Assessment

The leaders of the organization (or program) should explore the following questions before beginning work on a strategic message. The accumulation of answers of yes or no is less important than the discussion itself, which helps gauge whether the organization is ready to take this task on, and helps determine out how much the organization already knows about its goals, its approach to communication, and its constituents' desires.

Questions	Yes	No
1. Are we satisfied with how well people listen to us when we talk about our organization or program?		
2. Does everyone in our organization explain the overarching goal of the organization or program in the same way?		
3. Do we know who our target audiences are?		
4. Does everyone in the organization agree on the goal of the program or project we wish to communicate about?		
5. Can the group articulate the *action* we wish to have happen as a result of talking to stakeholders?		
6. When someone asks us to describe the purpose or the essence of the organization or program, can we do so effectively in less than thirty seconds?		
7. When we describe what we do or what our goal is, do people look at us blankly or with confusion when we are done?		
8. Can we talk about our program or project using *only* language that our next door neighbor would understand?		
9. Do we know what audiences we need to reach to achieve the goal of our organization or project?		
10. Do we know the desires of our audiences and what desires of theirs will be met if they take the action we want?		

Organizational Readiness Assessment

Ask yourself these questions to determine whether you are ready to develop a strategic message. Do not proceed until you can answer yes to every question.

Questions	Yes	No
1. Will we involve an interdisciplinary team in the message development process?		
2. Will the team include our organization's or program's leadership?		
3. Will we use the strategic message that is developed for a sustained period of time?		
4. Will we be disciplined about how we use the message, for example, refraining from changing it due to boredom?		
5. Will we commit to stating an organizational expectation that everyone in the organization, including board and volunteers, will learn to use the strategic message?		
6. Will we refrain from telling our audiences what they *should* want or do?		
7. Will we practice linking what we want them to do with something they desire?		

Endnotes

1 Ithiel de la Sola Pool et al., *Communications Flows: A Census in the United States and Japan* (Amsterdam: University of Tokyo Press, 1984), 33.

2 Gerald D. Bailey, Dan Lumley, and Deborah Dunbar, *Leadership & Technology: What School Board Members Need to Know* (Alexandria, VA: National School Boards Associations, 1995).

3 Peter Lyman and Hal R. Varian, "How Much Information," 2003. Retrieved from http://www.sims.berkeley.edu/how-much-info-2003 on 13 June 2005.

4 Duane E. Knapp, *The Brand Mindset* (New York: McGraw-Hill, 2000), 203.

5 Jeffery I. Cole, PhD, et al., *Surveying the Digital Future, Year Four: Ten Years, Ten Trends,* report from the Center for the Digital Future at USC Annenberg School, released September 2004, http://www.digitalcenter.org/downloads/DigitalFutureReport-Year4-2004.pdf.

6 M. Rex Miller, "The Digital Dynamic: How Communications Media Shape Our World," *The Futurist* vol. 39, no. 3, May/June 2005.

7 Ly Chheng, "E-mail worse for IQ than marijuana," *The Stanford Daily,* May 4, 2005, http://stanforddaily.com/tempo?page=content&repository=0001_article&id=17175.

8 Joel Garreau, "Point Men for a Revolution," *The Washington Post,* June 3, 1999.

9 GfK Roper Reports® US, 2000-Q1, GfK Roper Consulting.

10 Duane E. Knapp, *The Brand Mindset* (New York: McGraw-Hill, 2000), 75.

11 Frameworks Institute, "A Five-Minute Refresher Course in Framing," http://www.frameworksinstitute.org/products/issue8framing.shtml.

12 Stephen R. Covey, *Seven Habits of Highly Effective People* (New York: Simon & Shuster, 1990).

13 Peter Brinckerhoff, *Mission-Based Marketing: How Your Not-for-Profit Can Succeed in a More Competitive World* (Dillon, CO: Alpine Guild, 1997), 12.

14 John Kelly, "It's the Message That Counts, Answer Man Says," *The Washington Post,* August 13, 2006.

15 Dana Shelley, phone interview by author, November 21, 2005.

16 Stephen C. Rafe, *How to Be Prepared to Think on Your Feet* (New York: Harper Business, 1990), 74.

17 While the example is real, the organization's name is a pseudonym at the organization's request.

18 Sam Deep and Lyle Sussman, *What to Say to Get What You Want* (Cambridge, MA: Perseus Books, 1992), 108.

19 Fenton Communications, *Now Hear This: The Nine Laws of Successful Advocacy Communications,* publication funded by the David and Lucile Packard Foundation (Washington, DC, 2001), http://www.fenton.com/pages/5_resources/ nowhearthis.htm.

20 As noted previously, the example is real; the organization's name is a pseudonym at the organization's request.

21 Clayton M. Christensen, Scott Cook, and Taddy Hall, "Marketing Malpractice: The Cause and the Cure," *Harvard Business Review* vol. 83, no. 12 (December 2005).

22 Thea Lurie, interview by author, October 20, 2005.

23 The example is real; the professor's name was withheld at his request.

24 This survey was conducted in conjunction with creation of the *Communications Toolkit* (R. Christine Hershey, *Communications Toolkit: A Guide to Navigating Communications for the Nonprofit World,* Santa Monica, CA: Cause Communications, 2005). The survey was also referenced in a *Chronicle of Philanthropy* article (June 23, 2005, page 44) which cited the specific number from the survey as 62 percent. Underwriting foundations included the Annenberg Foundation, the California Endowment, the James Irvine Foundation, and the Marguerite Casey Foundation.

25 Ann Cramer, interview by author, October 10, 2005.

Index

c indicates chart
d indicates diagram

A

action
  awareness compared to, 45–46
  causing near-term, 18, 19
  disagreements about desired, 50–51
  example of identifying, 112, 115, 120
  identifying and articulating, 31–32,
    41–42, 49, 98–99, 129
  mission consistency with more than
    one, 42
  persuasion compared to, 45
  reaffirming, 82
  results from strategic messages, 11,
    14–15, 107–108
  self-interest drives, 32–33
  using different desires to motivate
    same, 63–67
Action Connection, 35*d*, 35–36, 40,
  43–44, 44*d*, 78*d*, 78–79
Action Connection framework
  as filter for new ideas, 128–130
  importance, 3, 127–128
  as tool for assessments, 131–132, 134
  as tool for executive management,
    127–128, 133–134
  as tool for focusing discussion, 134–135
  as tool for program development, 131–132
  as tool for revenue development, 132–133
alliances, forming, 114, 118
American Cancer Society, 57
American Lung Association (ALA), 28

Arlington Community Foundation, 87
asking organizational cultures, 71, 73
assessments
  Action Connection framework as tool
    for, 131–132, 134
  questionnaire for organizational needs,
    141
  questionnaire for organizational
    readiness, 142
  of success, 124–125
audiences
  addressing desires of individuals, 8–10
  clustering based on common desires,
    63–67
  core messages for, 15–16
  dropping part or all of one, 82
  identifying, 112, 115, 120
  internal, 70
  speaking to self-interest, 33
  testing assumptions about desires, 100
  working with varied, 123
  see also desires of audiences; target
    audiences
awareness and action, 45–47, 50–51

B

blogs, 69
board of directors. *See* leadership
brands/branding, 22–25, 27–28
brevity of message, 5, 37, 90

C

Center for the Study of Social Policy (CSSP)
    action as result of message, 107–108
    alliances, 114, 118
    background of, 109–111
    goals, 107
    message development process, 112, 115–116, 120
    message matrixes, 113, 117, 121–122
    success, 124–125
    target audiences, 56, 111
    using strategic message, 119
child abuse example, 86
    see also Center for the Study of Social Policy (CSSP)
child development example, 72–73
civic journalism, 10
common desires
    allocating resources for, 79–81, 82, 130
    clustering audiences by, 63–67
    identifying, 112, 116, 120
    mutual satisfaction compared to, 77
    strategic message focuses on, 14
    of target audiences and organization, 35*d*, 35–36, 40, 43–44, 44*d*, 78*d*, 78–79
communications
    amount, 7–8
    importance, 4
    oral, 29
    organization's department of, 48, 50
    resources, 58–59
    revolution, 4
    speed, 1, 8
    sustaining, 35*d*, 35–36
consistency, importance of, 16
consultants. *See* facilitators
core messages
    and consistency, 16
    creating, 112, 116, 120
    described, 15–16
    drafts, 102
    example of one targeting different audiences, 66, 91

core messages (*continued*)
    examples, 19, 28, 49, 86
    examples for identity building, 22, 87
    examples with subset messages, 17*c*, 113*c*, 117*c*, 121*c*
    length, 90
    limiting number of points, 37
    purpose, 28
    slogans compared to, 28

D

data gathering, 69–70, 100
decision making, 8, 10–11
deliverers of message
    example of message not created by, 121–122
    and length of message, 29, 37–38
    and message matrix, 104
    staying focused, 7
desires
    addressing individual, 8–10
    determining, 69–74, 74*c*, 75
    motivating same action by different, 63–67
    trump needs, 68–69
    see also common desires
desires of audiences
    focusing on, 34
    identifying, 99–100, 101, 130
    identifying, examples of, 112, 115, 120
    and mission statements, 20
    reflected in message, 11
    testing assumptions about, 100
diabetes research example, 21–22, 46
Doris Duke Charitable Foundation, 109, 110
drinking and driving, 42

E

Edna McConnell Clark Foundation, 89
elevator speeches, 29
evaluations. *See* assessments
executives. *See* leadership

F

facilitators
  importance, 105
  tasks, 97–98, 100
  using outside, 27, 51
  writing skills, 98
flexible language, importance of, 22, 29
focus groups, 69, 72
frames/framing, 25–27
fundraising strategic message, 19

G

goals
  achieving, 14
  of CSSP, 107
  of frames, 26
  identifying, 31–32, 41–42
  link between articulating and funding,
    132
  and strategic message development
    process, 6
  of strategic messages, 26–27
graphic identity elements, 22–23, 25

H

health and human services delivery
  example, 66–67
higher education example, 134–135

I

idea filters, 128–130
identity-building strategic messages
  and awareness, 46
  brands/branding compared to, 22–24,
    25
  examples, 21–22, 87
  and mission statement, 20
  slogans compared to, 27
informal focus groups, 69
information
  gathering, 69–70, 100
  overload, 42
  processing ability, 38, 39*c*

J

jargon, 88–89, 111
The Jargon Files (web site), 89
journalism examples, 19, 46
Juvenile Diabetes Foundation (JDF), 21
Juvenile Diabetes Research Foundation
  International, 21–22, 46

K

Knight Journalism Initiative, 46

L

Lake Street Church, 57
Langford, Judy, 124
language
  brevity, 37, 90
  changes necessary in organizational
    materials, 104–105
  creating for strategic message, 103
  creating frames, 26
  flexible, 22, 29, 92
  jargon, 88–89, 111
  to resonate with target audiences, 85,
    87, 92
  validating, 118
leadership
  Action Connection framework as
    management tool for, 127–128,
    133–134
  involvement in strategic message
    development, 96
  and organizational culture, 73
less is more rule, 38, 39*c*, 58, 90
listservs, 69
logos, 22–23, 25
lung diseases example, 28

M

marketing orientations, 74
market research, 23, 69–70, 100, 101
medical center marketing example, 91
me orientation, 6

message matrixes
CSSP example, 113, 117, 121–122
described, 16–17
drafts, 100, 103
finalizing, 104
messages. *See* core messages; strategic
messages; subset messages
mission
achieving, 2
clarity, 47–48
different actions consistent with, 42
understanding, 49
mission statements, 20, 47
Mothers Against Drunk Driving
(MADD), 42
mutual desires. *See* common desires
mutual satisfaction, 6, 77

N

National Alliance of Children's Trust
and Prevention Funds, 114
National Association for the Education of
Young Children (NAEYC), 86, 114
Nebraska Health and Human Services
System (NHHSS), 66–67
needs
assessment of organization's, 141
desires trump, 68–69
focusing on, 34
New Funders for Journalism Reform, 19

O

observational market research, 69–70
oral communications, 29
organizational identity
and awareness, 46
and brands/branding, 22–24, 25
developing clearer, 18, 20, 21–22
examples, 21–22, 87
and slogans, 27
organizations
adopting mind-set of strategic message,
138–139
assessment of needs, 141

organizations (*continued*)
assessment of readiness, 142
changes in, 6
cultures of, 71–74
desire overlap with audiences, 35*d*,
35–36, 40, 43–44, 44*d*, 78*d*,
78–79
identifying desire overlap with
audiences example, 112, 116, 120
involvement in strategic message
development, 47, 48, 50
shared internal priorities, 80–81

P

personal power, 8–11
persuasion and frames, 26
persuasion *vs.* action, 45
point of view, 85–87
political/public policy issues and frames, 26
programs
Action Connection framework as tool
for developing, 131–132
necessity of changes in, 79–81, 82
Proscio, Tony, 89
"the public," 54–56

R

repetition, importance of, 16
resources
Action Connection framework as tool
for developing, 132–133
allocating, 49, 129, 130
dedicated, 109, 110
fundraising strategic message, 19
necessary for creating brands *vs.*
strategic messages, 25
reallocating to achieve common
desires, 79–81, 82
rule of three, 38, 39*c*, 58, 90

S

sales orientations, 74
self-interest
drives action, 32–33
drives listening, 61–63, 67

shared desires. *See* common desires
slogans, 27–28
social movements, 123–124
St. Mary's Community Foundation, 57
State Government Management
    Initiative (SGMI), 49, 64–65
strategic message development process
    benefits, 6
    challenges, 139
    facilitators, 97–98, 105
    identifying desired action, 31–32,
        41–42, 50–51
    logistics, 97
    meeting interludes, 100, 103
    meetings, 98–100, 102–104, 105
    organizational involvement, 47, 48, 50
    steps, 43–44, 44*d*, 52
    steps, examples of, 112, 115–116, 120
    team members, 2, 95–97, 105
strategic messages
    benefits, 6, 7, 11, 30
    defined, 14–15
    elements of successful, 38, 39*c*, 85–93
    elevator speeches compared to, 29
    goals, 26–27
    measuring success, 6
    mission statements compared to, 47
    need for, 2, 18–22, 138
    not created by deliverers, 121–122
    and social movements, 123–124
    using, 105, 106, 119
    see also identity-building strategic
        messages
subset messages
    creating, examples of, 112, 116, 120
    described, 15–16
    drafts, 100, 102
    for each target audience, 101
    examples with core message, 17*c*,
        66–67, 113*c*, 117*c*, 121*c*
    finalizing, 103, 104
    repetition in, 16
surveys, 69, 72

T
tactical tools, 47
target audiences
    capturing attention of, 61–63, 67,
        85–89, 92, 130
    changing, 56
    as channels, 57–58
    of CSSP, 56, 111
    defined, 53
    example identifying overlap of
        organization desires with those of,
        112, 116, 120
    identifying, 99
    identifying desires of, 99–100, 101, 130
    limiting number, 37, 58–59
    message for different, 66, 91
    motivating, 43
    overlap of organization desires with
        those of, 35*d*, 35–36, 40, 43–44,
        44*d*, 78*d*, 78–79
    and resource allocation, 129
    sizes of, 54–56
    subset messages for each, 101
    subsets, 15–16
    target markets compared to, 55
target markets, 55
technology
    and expectations, 1
    medium *vs.* message, 7
    speed of change, 8
telling organizational cultures, 71

V
vision statements. *See* mission statements
visuals, 22–23, 25

W
Wilderness Society, 57

Z
ZERO TO THREE, 72–73

More results-oriented books from Fieldstone Alliance

Fieldstone Alliance Nonprofit Guide to
Crafting Effective Mission and Vision Statements

Too often, if you ask four people in a nonprofit what their organization's mission is, you'll get four different answers. This book will guide your organization through a six-step process that results in a mission statement, vision statement, or both. Includes sample mission and vision statements, step-by-step instructions, and worksheets.

by Emil Angelica   Item #06927X   88 pages

The Lobbying and Advocacy Handbook
for Nonprofit Organizations

This guide will help you understand your nonprofit's role in shaping public policy, assess the benefits of lobbying to fulfill your mission, and show you how to develop and carry out an advocacy plan.

by Marcia Avner   Item #069261   240 pages

Mobilize People for Marketing Success

How to mobilize your entire organization, its staff, volunteers, and supporters in a focused one-to-one marketing campaign. This unique guide gives you complete instructions, real-life examples, and detailed worksheets to create an effective campaign.

by Gary J. Stern   Item #069105   208 pages

Strengthening Nonprofit Performance
A Funder's Guide to Capacity Building

A collection of strategies, steps, and examples that funders can use to get started on or improve their funding to strengthen nonprofits.

by Paul Connolly and Carol Lukas   Item #069377   184 pages